A SHORTER COMMENT

A SHORTER COMMENTARY ON ROMANS

*

KARL BARTH

WIPF & STOCK · Eugene, Oregon

Wipf and Stock Publishers
199 W 8th Ave, Suite 3
Eugene, OR 97401

A Shorter Commentary on Romans
By Barth, Karl
Copyright©1960 SCM
ISBN 13: 978-1-62032-526-1
Publication date 10/1/2012
Previously published by SCM, 1960

Contents

5

Preface

THIS *Shorter Commentary on Romans* is a smaller and younger (though already fairly old) brother of the *Epistle to the Romans* of 1918 and 1921. It originated as the manuscript for a course of extra-mural lectures, held in Basle during the winter of 1940-1. In these lectures the characteristic suspense in which we too lived in those days will hardly be noticed. I would just mention the unusual fact that I gave some of them – those on Rom. 8, I seem to remember – in a rather weather-beaten uniform of the Auxiliary Armed Forces. But otherwise, just as in Bonn in 1933, I was determined to continue 'as if nothing had happened'. Since then various copies of the manuscript have come into existence. Until now I have resisted the request to have it published but now the demand has brought such pressure to bear on me that I have overcome my objections. Here therefore is what was demanded.

This really is a *short* commentary on Romans. In many places the need for supplementary information from other commentaries will force itself on the reader. Those who want to read more from my pen about the Epistle to the Romans will now as before have to have recourse to that older book or to my later writings, especially the *Church Dogmatics*. It stands to reason that this text has continued to influence me also in other respects. In the footnotes, at least in some major parts, will be found references to my continued efforts in other places to do greater justice to the text, and it will be found that what is said in this book has to some extent already been superseded elsewhere. After all, there is always something new to learn from the Epistle to the Romans. In this sense (once again using my rather bold expression of the preface of 1918) it is certainly still 'waiting' for me too!

Much could be said about the relationship as regards language, method and contents between this and the older book, or the two older books respectively. It will be seen at the first glance that this is not an extract from the older exposition. I expect a few critics will have something to say about this. I shall spare them and the other readers the comments I myself could make on it. In both cases it was my intention – and it will remain my intention in future, if I again have to say something about the Epistle to the Romans – to let Paul speak for himself. No interpreter could escape from the qualification: 'as I understand him', and that naturally applies to me too. But I did and do hope that Paul is strong enough to make himself heard even through the medium of interpretations which are still and ever remain inadequate.

One more remark. I advised those attending the lectures, inasmuch as they knew no Greek, to follow my expositions in a modern translation[1] (Weizsaecker, Schlatter, Zuericher Bibel, Menge). Unfortunately I have no time to provide the readers of this book with the text as I would now translate it in a coherent rendering which is at the same time faithful and readable. I must therefore ask them to consult one of those other translations whilst reading this book – at any rate my own of 1918 and 1921 which I did not want to reproduce here.

Basle, *February* 1956

---

[1] *Translator's Note :* The English reader will find the Revised Version very reliable. However, he would do well to consult a good *modern* English translation too, e.g. Weymouth, Moffatt, Revised Standard Version or Phillips.

Introduction and Summary

THE Epistle to the Romans really is a letter – or rather an epistle – to the Christian Church in Rome, written in Greek by the Apostle Paul, whom we also know from the Acts of the Apostles and by a number of similar epistles. There is reason to assume that he wrote, or rather, dictated it to a certain Tertius (16.22) in Corinth in A.D. 58, and that Phoebe, the deaconess mentioned in 16.1, took it to Rome. It therefore dates from a later time than the two Epistles to the Thessalonians, the Epistle to the Galatians and the two Epistles to the Corinthians, which it precedes in the New Testament, but it is older than any of the other writings which the NT has preserved under Paul's name.

We do not know by whom, at what date or in what circumstances the Church in Rome was founded. According to 1.6 we may assume that it mainly consisted of members who had been Gentiles. Not a few of these, according to the list of greetings in Chapter 16, had their original homes in the east of the Roman empire. All the contents of the Epistle show that the OT was read diligently in the Church (there was of course no NT at the time) and that its proper interpretation offered a serious problem to the Church. This may be connected with questions suggested by the existence of the Jewish synagogue in Rome, or perhaps with the kind of questions a certain group among the Christians who had been Jews would ask wherever there were Christian Churches.

When (1.8) the Apostle says that the whole world knows about the faith of the Christians in Rome, and when he says so

9

emphatically in 1.10ff that for a time now he has been yearning to visit them, this is an indication of the importance possessed by that Church simply because its home was in the capital of the Empire and of the world: and that it had consequently already gained part of that key position which it was to acquire in the subsequent centuries and has retained ever since. Peter may have been in Rome afterwards, as the Roman Catholic tradition, supported by distinguished Protestant scholars, maintains, and he may have been executed there. Nevertheless, in this Epistle we are dealing with an even older document of the history of that Church. It should also be noted that in the later Epistles which he wrote from Rome (e.g. in the Epistle to the Philippians) Paul refers to his Christian environment in the city in a very reserved way, to put it mildly, and that these epistles show no trace of Peter's presence in Rome. Besides, a rather sharp but undefined warning against false teachers which threaten the inner life of the Church in Rome is already to be found at the end of this Epistle (16.17-20).

Why did Paul write this Epistle? We learn from 15.22ff that he is on his way from Macedonia and Greece to Jerusalem, there to hand over the collection in aid of the Mother Church, which was discussed in detail in II Cor. As he regards his task in the eastern part of the Empire as finished (15.19, 23), he now intends to travel, via Rome, to Spain, to continue his missionary work there. Paul was by reputation a well-known man throughout the Christian world of his time, but as he once said himself (II Cor. 6.8): 'By honour and dishonour, by evil report and good report.'

He had many adversaries, not only among Jews and Gentiles but also in the Christian Church itself. What with all that he said and particularly with the way in which he said, wrote or dictated it, he was not only far from easy to bear with but to many good – or not so good – Christians a real cause of offence. No doubt he quite deliberately interfered in person whenever he thought it necessary – and that was quite frequently. Why and how he had to defend himself becomes powerfully manifest

in the Epistle to the Galatians, for instance. And how he himself was criticized, even if it was done very kindly, we may,
perhaps with a little smile, read in II Peter 3.15f.

This controversial and argumentative man now intended to
travel to Rome, and he therefore considered it necessary and
right to introduce himself to the Christians there. They had
to learn from Paul himself – not who and what he was personally, but what were his office and his message. They were to
get to know his presentation of the Gospel with its definite
concentration on the question of the *proper interpretation of the
Old Testament*, which was evidently very much on their minds –
and not only on theirs. This was also the great theme of his
own life, the life of the man who had been a Jewish scribe and
had become a Christian missionary. It was the theme around
which the controversies moved which he aroused in the Church
and had to overcome, and consequently it was undoubtedly the
most suitable theme if he wanted to introduce himself, or rather
not himself but his cause, to people who so far only knew him
from hearsay. When he wrote this Epistle, he evidently expected that a comprehensive statement on this theme would be
his best introduction to the Church in Rome; and this introduction he needed for the carrying out of his further plans in
the west of the Empire. We do not know to what extent his
expectations were fulfilled. After all, Paul eventually arrived in
Rome in an entirely different way from the one he had expected:
his best introduction to the Church in Rome; and this intro-
ducing himself and his cause that he wrote the Epistle to the
Romans.

And with that we have already stated the essential thing
about its contents. It has often been compared to a catechism,
or even to a handbook of dogmatics, and for that reason the
first systematic theologian of the Evangelical Church, Melanch-
thon, did in fact use it as a pattern for a work of this kind.
There is some truth in that impression, for the Epistle to the
Romans does in fact contain a greater element of doctrine and
a more systematic development and exposition of the Christian

faith than any other writing of the NT. We ought however to bear in mind that it differs from a catechism or a manual of dogmatics. Its particular aim (particularly towards the end of the Epistle this aim was not always pursued with the utmost tenacity, but on the whole it stands out extremely clearly) is the one which Luther in his preface to the Epistle has marked with unerring precision: 'That is why it appears as if in this Epistle St Paul desires to give a short summary of the whole of Christian and evangelical doctrine and provide an access to the whole of the Old Testament. For there is no doubt that he who carries this Epistle in his heart carries the light and power of the Old Testament with him. Every Christian ought therefore to know this Epistle and study it persistently.' But this aim meant that the exposition of Christian doctrine, which admittedly we do find in this Epistle, does not reach that external perfection which should be the mark of a catechism or a handbook of dogmatics. In any case the contents of the Epistle to the Romans are, in shortest outline, as follows.

In the Introduction, 1.1-17, Paul comments on his office and on the Gospel he proclaims as such. The Gospel, which was already proclaimed in the OT and which primarily therefore (1.16) applies to the Jews, is about Jesus Christ the Son of God, who was born as a descendant of David and is risen from the dead. He himself has sent Paul as his messenger to all the Gentiles. And, consequently, those in Rome who had once been Gentiles, are also within the scope of his mandate. The Introduction ends with the statement that in the Gospel the disclosure of the divine judgment upon all the world takes place, but that the faith which accepts this judgment and submits to it is every man's salvation and life.

1.18–3.20 form another distinct unit. With constant reference to that which the OT has already attested, Paul shows that in the Gospel, and therefore in the message concerning Jesus Christ, a divine judgment is in fact pronounced, a negative judgment on all men: a condemnation of Jews and Gentiles alike. But according to what is set forth in the next major division of the

Epistle (3.21–8.39) this aspect changes, when – again under the guidance of the OT – we take into consideration that this judgment of God, by which all are condemned, is pronounced in Jesus Christ, executed by his death, and therefore acquits and justifies all those who believe in him. So that, if it is heard and received in faith, the Gospel as the disclosure of this judgment is indeed a Gospel; not bad but good news. It is the message of reconciliation between God and man, and of man's new life in righteousness, in freedom, under the guidance of the Spirit.

Chapters 9-11 then explain what the Gospel means in the place where it should have found belief in the first place but where in fact it has not been believed: among the Jews of the Synagogue, who, although they have the Old Testament, the Gospel's decisive testimony, in their hands, evidently have not yet understood it. This is matched in 12.1–15.13 in a series of exhortations with an indication of what the Gospel means in practice in the place where it has been believed; in the Church of Jesus Christ of which the church in Rome must be counted a part. The final chapters (15.14–16.27) consist of the personal communications we have already mentioned, a number of greetings to and from several people, that rather abrupt warning against false teachers (16.17-18) and a solemn praise of the God who has revealed himself in the Gospel (16.25-27). These are the main points of the Epistle to the Romans, which we shall have to work out in more detail in these lectures.

One more comment for the sake of completeness. Only a very few nineteenth-century scholars have seriously doubted that the Apostle Paul really is the author of the Epistle to the Romans and that we are therefore not dealing here with one of the forgeries which in those centuries were quite a respectable literary practice. It really cannot be doubted unless we are prepared to regard all the Pauline Epistles as second-century forgeries. But that is out of the question, if only because, according to all that we know about it, the spiritual climate of that later period was notoriously entirely different from the one which comes to light in the Pauline Epistles and thus also in the

Epistle to the Romans. There is some doubt about the end of the Epistle, from 15.1 onward, for it is probable that in about A.D. 200 there were in existence some Latin translations of the Epistle, which ended with 14.23 – in which that end was therefore missing.

Marcion, the famous heretic, also affirmed that he knew the Epistle only in this shorter form, though it is true that he was in the habit of taking more than the usual liberties in dealing with the text of the NT. However, we can see at a glance that the discussion of the theme of Chapter 14 is continued without a break in Chapter 15, so that we should not attach too much importance to this problem though it certainly does exist. On the other hand there are serious reasons for assuming that the doxology in 16.25-27 may not have been an original part of the Epistle but may have been added afterwards. Another question is whether Chapter 16, especially with its many greetings to people personally known to Paul, could not be explained more easily on the assumption that, while Paul is the author, it originally formed part of an epistle written by him to the Church in Ephesus. The arguments for and against this hypothesis are more or less evenly divided. It is and remains very possible that this chapter too belongs to the integral text of the Epistle to the Romans. We are in good company if we notice this problem but leave it open and apply ourselves to the text as it is presented to us by the overwhelming majority of the textual evidence, and as in fact it has always been read by the Christian Church.

The Apostolic Office and the Gospel

THE arrangement of these verses, which form the Introduction to the whole Epistle, is clear: 1.1-7, the Apostle's greetings to his readers in Rome; 1.8-15, a note on his wish to come to Rome soon himself; 1.16-18, a programmatic definition of the Gospel as the disclosure of God's judgment, which to the man who accepts it in faith becomes salvation and life.

1.1-7 contain the author's greetings in the form which was then usual. He mentions his own name and the name of those he is addressing, and then in direct speech wishes them the best he can wish them. But in this traditional form Paul has at once spoken very substantially of the cause that moves him. This cause is a person (1.1), not his own person, nor the person of the individual reader or hearer of the Epistle, but over and above his person and the persons united in the church in Rome the person of Jesus Christ. Paul is his servant, literally his slave, that is to say to him he belongs and he wishes to speak only as one who belongs to him, and not privately and in his own right. When he was called by him, called away from his previous surroundings, and also from his previous inner and outer position in life, and by this was set apart to be an apostle, he became this same Lord's personal property. This Lord has given him the grace of the apostolate (1.5), i.e. the office of an accredited ambassador, and this office commissions him to proclaim the Gospel, the good news.

Paul is now separated from everything in the world, tied entirely to the Gospel, set apart for the Gospel – and that by Jesus Christ, the One of whom he would say in 1.3f that he is the content of the Gospel. But he first of all wants to emphasize (1.2) that this good news is identical with that which the prophets have already asserted in the Holy Scriptures (he means those of Israel: the Old Testament). They have declared the good news beforehand. They announced it before it was there to take its course through the world by means of the Apostle's words. Therefore these Scriptures should be read as announcements exactly corresponding to the Gospel. The content of the Gospel is only One – and whatever may appear to be otherwise is yet this One: the Son of God. According to the flesh, i.e. as a man he belongs to the house of David, he is the son and heir promised to David. According to the Holy Spirit, through his resurrection from the dead, i.e. through his power as the Son of God, he has been appointed, i.e. proved, revealed, lit. set apart and distinguished from other men as just this: the Son of God. Jesus Christ is Paul's Lord. And from him Paul has received (1.5) the grace of his commission to call all the Gentiles to obedience to the King of Israel because he is as such the Son of God who is above all men – to call them to that obedience which consists in faith, so that through their obedience his Name (the name of Jesus Christ as the Son of God and the son of David) may receive due honour. His readers originally belonged to those Gentiles – but, like Paul himself they were 'called in Jesus Christ', in their particular situation called away (1.6): they are 'all the beloved of God, those who were called, the saints in Rome' (1.7).

What is true of what Paul says about himself also applies here: none of these epithets indicates a religious moral quality of those thus described. They point to Christ's work for them and to them. Through him they are God's beloved, called by him, holy through him, in exactly the same way and in the same sense as Paul is an Apostle through him. Thus Jesus Christ is their unity, the One in whom the Apostle and the Church, right from the start, without ever having seen each other, simply are together. In this unity the Apostle greets the Church with a blessing. While the Greeks and Romans of those days wished each other 'joy' and 'prosperity' the Apostle wishes his readers 'grace' and 'peace'. We shall meet those words again, so that it may be sufficient here to state that they indicate, so to speak from above and from below, that which makes the Church the Church, which makes a Christian a Christian: God's favourable inclination towards man, and the order of human life which is the result of that inclination. In Jesus Christ grace and peace have become an event and are yet ever to be expected and therefore to be solicited from him who is the fountain of grace and peace: from God our Father, whom we have recognized as our Father through Jesus Christ – from our Lord Jesus Christ who as such is the way to God our Father. The more we keep the two words of this phrase together, the more clearly we can see that the one can only be explained by the other, and the better we understand them.

In 1.8-15 Paul comments on his wish personally to meet with the Church in Rome. He begins as he usually does by thanking God for the existence of the Church (1.8). There is perhaps no more telling expression of the peculiar character of the apostolic office as distinguished from that of the priests and prophets in the OT than this thanksgiving which is regularly the Apostle's first word as regards his Churches. When he addresses himself to God through and in Jesus Christ he may, he must extol the mere existence of a Christian church as a miracle of God's goodness. For the faith of the Christians in Rome to which he is referring in particular and which he says is known throughout the world, is certainly not their sincere, their deep, their live faith, but just their faith as such: just the fact that Jesus Christ has saints, his disciples – and this is significant for the whole world – in Rome too. While Paul, remembering them in this sense, turns to God, it stands to reason – and he can call upon God to bear him out (1.9) – that he prays for them, that in this strictest sense of the word they are near to his heart. And his intercession for them quite naturally becomes a prayer that it may be God's will for him to come to them one day. He would (1.11) like to see them in order to strengthen them by passing on to them the gift of the Spirit bestowed on him.

This particular gift of the Spirit is simply the Gospel, which according to 1.5 has been entrusted to him. Other men have other gifts. In I Cor. 12 Paul spoke of the diversity of spiritual gifts, and in this Epistle too he discussed them (12.6ff). This particular gift, the proclamation of the Gospel, is the gift of the apostolic office bestowed on him. In all his epistles Paul emphasized its importance not only for the foundation of the Church (i.e. for missions in the narrower sense of the world), but also for strengthening, building and maintaining her.

But the apostolic office does not make the man who holds it self-satisfied. Therefore, as he continues, Paul adds that to him strengthening them is synonymous with hoping that he will be comforted and exhorted with them by the mutual exchange of their faith and his. He takes it seriously that Jesus Christ is over him and the rest of the Church, and that he, Paul himself is not over and above the Church but lives in the Church, receiving as well as giving.

Therefore, when he prays for the Church in Rome and pleads that he may be allowed to see her, he is praying for himself as well. He has so far been prevented from carrying out his desire (1.13). According to 1.10 Paul is convinced that, if it could not be carried out so far, it was evidently not the will of God – this is in keeping with his usual interpretation of such situations. But they are to know that from his side the desire and the intention had always been there – now his third motive appears – to 'have some fruit', harvest some produce in Rome, as well as among the other Gentiles, i.e. to preach the Gospel as a missionary there as well, to win some people for the good news, to guide some people to that obedience of faith mentioned in 1.5. Whenever Paul speaks of Gentile nations and their being won for the Gospel, he always means *some few* people from those nations, as is very plain in this sentence. In those few the nations as a whole are the objects of his commission, the hearers of his message. Paul's idea of mission is not concerned with large or small numbers. What really matters is this: that the spark, and in the spark the future conflagration of the whole, is scattered throughout the world.

Finally 1.14-15 may be understood as the intimation of a fourth motive for his desire to come to Rome. For Paul explains that desire (once more mentioned explicitly in 1.15) by his specific calling to a world-wide apostolate, to a proclamation of the Gospel among Hellenes and Barbarians, among the educated and the uneducated. Originally the Greeks were the Hellenes and, in Greek idiom, all the other nations Barbarians. But by the time this Epistle was written the words had acquired a different nuance of meaning. 'Hellenic' was the embodiment of culture, 'barbarian' was the opposite. The two words used in conjunction by a Christian who was once a Jew denoted the non-Jewish, i.e. the Gentile world in its entirety and in its diversity. He was directed to serve the Gospel as the Apostle of the Gentile world, as distinguished from those Apostles who, now as before, continued in Jerusalem to perform the same office among the Jews. That is his task and it is the fourth reason why he wishes to go to Rome. Rome is the centre of the hellenic-barbarian world of the Gentiles, with its mixture of the highest civilization and the lowest vulgarity. But when we look back at this whole exposition in 1.8-15 we should remember that the actual nerve, the decisive force of this desire is located at the place where Paul sees that he is together and at one with the Christians in Rome as well as with those of other churches – however wide apart in space and however unknown to each other they may be – in the unity of Jesus Christ, who is at once both his, the Lord of the Apostle and theirs, the Lord of the Church.

The last phrases of the introduction give a definition (1.16-17) of what Paul means by the Gospel which he has just said once more he intends to preach in Rome (1.15). In these verses he begins to present the cause for which the Epistle was written. But the transition from what precedes them is scarcely noticeable.

Paul starts by saying in 1.16 that he is *not ashamed* of the Gospel. This certainly refers to what he has said before: that for a long time now he had wanted to come to Rome, but had not yet managed to do so. No one should think that he could not or would not come because he shunned the challenge which Rome especially, as the impressive centre of the Gentile world, would mean to his message. He is not afraid that the Gospel might not be equal to its encounter with the accumulated culture and vulgarity of the metropolis, that the spiritual and unspiritual powers, the culture and banality prevailing there might confound the Gospel and stultify him as well. But this 'shamelessness' is not based on any reliance on his own spiritual resources, on his eloquence, on his knowledge of human nature or anything of that kind. The reason why he is 'shameless', why he is not afraid of all Rome – and here he arrives at the cause which will be his sole concern till 15.13 – is because the Gospel itself is *power*; it is *God's* power and therefore in every respect superior power.

Observe how he refrains from making any reference to his own conviction or experience of this power. And also note that he does not say that the Gospel *has* such power (as if it might perhaps not have it). On the contrary, he states – we shall have to get used to the fact that this is how an apostle speaks – that the Gospel *is* such power. The phrase means that it is God's almighty power, God's omnipotence. It is therefore not a power among other powers, it is not a power to which others could even be compared, it is not a power with which another power could compete, but the power which is over and above all other powers, which limits and governs them all. That is the Gospel. How could it then be confounded in that large and yet very small city of Rome? How then could its messenger be ashamed?

We have already learned in 1.4 that the person of Jesus Christ is the content of the Gospel. The ancient copyist who inserted this name in the text has therefore not made any real alteration. Paul was of course thinking of this content and

20

therefore of this person of the Gospel, when he called it God's almighty power. Wherever Jesus Christ is the content, every form assumes his nature. But the nature of Jesus Christ is God's omnipotence. That is how the Gospel came to be God's omnipotence.

But what is this almighty power of God? Paul has a very definite view on the matter: God's omnipotence, ultimately the only power in the world, is the power which is active 'unto salvation to everyone who believes, to the Jew first and also to the Greek'. These words are best read without disrupting their context. Paul knows of a work that has been set in motion and that will irresistibly remain in motion. This work consists in *salvation*. This work reaches its aim in *everyone who believes* by the fact that they are saved by it. And this work takes its course first to the *Jews*, and from there to the *Greeks*, i.e. to the Gentile nations in the region of the Mediterranean, which were then under the sway of Greek language and civilization. It takes this course so that in the faith of the Jews first and then of the Greeks it reaches its aim and they are saved. Consequently, God's omnipotence is the power which is active in this work of salvation. And conversely, what is active in this work is in the strictest sense of the word God's almighty power. Much of what follows becomes more intelligible, if we remember that this identification is part of Paul's ABC. He was never to write even a sentence on the assumption that there was any doubt about this identification. So let us make a mental note that the Gospel is this almighty work of salvation.

And now, in 1.17 we learn very briefly what Paul means when he calls the Gospel this work of salvation. A *revelation* takes place in the Gospel. That simply means the uncovering, the disclosure of something which otherwise is and must remain hidden. Here as well as later in 1.18 Paul speaks in the present tense. We cannot look back on the revelation in the Gospel as on other historical events. The revelation does not stop taking place in the Gospel. We cannot hear the Gospel without becoming a contemporary, a witness of that which happens in it. The revelation which takes place in the Gospel is the revelation of *God's righteousness*, i.e. the just verdict of God the Judge. That which otherwise is and remains hidden but becomes visible in the Gospel is the 'judgment-seat' (II Cor. 5.10), occupied by the Man, whom God, after his overlooking of the times of ignorance, has appointed to judge the whole world, the quick and the dead in righteousness. (Acts 10.42; 17.30f). For this Man, Jesus Christ, is the content of the Gospel. He is revealed in the Gospel and God's verdict is revealed in him. The hearer of the Gospel becomes his contemporary, a witness to the revelation. And he who pronounces God's verdict also completes that almighty work of salvation. That is the second amazing identification in these verses: God's verdict is God's work of salvation. The Judge is the Saviour. When Paul acknowledges the Gospel as God's power of salvation, he has the Man in view, through whom God reveals his verdict, and abides by this verdict.

The words 'by faith unto faith' (RV) added here are not exactly easy to understand. The most likely interpretation seems to be that they are a play on words. The Greek word for 'faith' (*pistis*) means faithfulness as well as trust.[1] In 3.3 it is actually used to indicate God's faithfulness, and we shall have to allow for the possibility that in other places as well it may express not man's faith but God's faithfulness. If this were to be assumed here then everything becomes clear: the verdict pronounced by Jesus Christ has its origin in God's faithfulness, it is the word of God's faithfulness, and it aims at the trust, the faith of the Jewish and Greek people who hear it. In view of that origin and that aim of its revelation this verdict really is what Paul calls it: God's almighty work of salvation. *'The righteous by faith'*, who according to the concluding quotation from Hab. 2.4 shall *live*, is the Jew or Greek who has heard the Gospel in such a way that God's verdict contained in it, and therefore God's almighty work of salvation, has achieved its

---

[1] Keeping faith *with* someone as well as having faith *in* someone. *Translator.*

end with him – the Jew or the Greek who believes by accepting the verdict and confessing that he is the man whom the divine verdict means and concerns. The man who does that, who with heart and tongue submits to God's verdict, really believes and stands with his faith before God as one who is right in his sight. He precisely is the one who shall live, he shall receive salvation, and through his salvation that life which God's verdict has awarded him.

It should be mentioned however that there has been a Greek translation of that saying of Habakkuk's, which was perhaps not unknown to Paul, according to which it should read: 'The righteous shall live by *my* [God's] faithfulness. Neither is it impossible that Paul, in speaking of the man of whom that was said, originally and primarily did not think of the hearer and receiver of the Gospel, but of the One who is its content, i.e. the man Jesus Christ, the righteous Judge appointed by the faithful God, whose life, i.e. whose resurrection from the dead (1.4), is that revelation, already prophesied in the OT, which Paul is now going to explain. Without Jesus Christ in the background it is certainly not possible to understand what is said in the foreground, here and in everything that follows, about the man who believes. *His* righteousness is that of the faithful God and therefore that of the man who trusts in him. And his life, saved from death, is the life promised to the man who has become righteous through him. The proclamation of this righteousness and this life, the proclamation of the faith which causes man to participate in this righteousness and this life, that is the apostolic office to which Paul has been appointed, and in pursuit of which he wrote the Epistle to the Romans.

The Gospel as God's Condemnation of Man

DOES Paul mean a second or even a first revelation apart from the one mentioned in 1.17 when now he suddenly introduces a *revelation* of God's *wrath* about all the ungodliness (irreverence) and iniquity (insubordination) of men, viz. of the Gentiles (1.18-32) and the Jews (2.1–3.20)? Has he abandoned his office as a messenger of the Gospel for a while in order to speak in the first place in an entirely different capacity as a religious interpreter of the human situation as such, as a Christian philosopher of religion and history? This section has often been interpreted as if this were the case. Then that whole rather long section 1.18–3.20 would mean that Paul – as bad preachers are admittedly in the habit of doing – is leading off with a lengthy discussion of something quite different from his text, i.e. from the matter which he has already indicated clearly and unmistakably.

Can we regard him as capable of that? There is certainly no external evidence of any such change of front right at the beginning of the Epistle. Moreover it is definitely impossible to understand what is said about the Jews in 2.1 ff. if one does not realize that Paul is not speaking from a general, human point of view, but from the viewpoint of the Gospel; that the divine judgment there pronounced is that which the Gospel preaches to the Jews, and that consequently Paul is unmistakably speaking as an apostle.

But if that is so, why should it be assumed that he would take up a different attitude when he speaks in Chapter 1 about the Gentiles? To which other 'revelation of God from heaven' could he possibly refer when in these verses he wants to develop the theme, summed up at the end of this section and the beginning of the next, in these words: 'We have proved both Jews and Gentiles guilty, that they are all under the dominion of sin' (3.9). '. . . so that every mouth may be stopped and all the world become guilty before God' (3.19). 'There is no distinction: they have all sinned and come short of glory before God' (3.23; 'come short of the glory of God' EVV?) Ought the words 'from heaven' to suggest another source of this revelation? But which source could it possibly be, since we have learned that the Gospel itself is God's almighty power and therefore presumably the sum total of all heavenly majesty? And what Paul puts forward as the content of this revelation no one has ever yet said, or has even been able to say or repeat, unless he was expounding that very revelation of which Paul has spoken before: that divine verdict pronounced by the man Jesus. Belief in the Gospel alone will accept those statements, this whole discourse on God's wrath, and not contradict it. But that means that already in this chapter we are not in a kind of outer court, but right in the heart of the matter. The verdict of the faithful God on the whole world, which is revealed in Jesus Christ, has this side, this dark side as well: it is also the revelation of God's wrath. And if this happens not to agree with our educational views, then it is all the more significant for the Apostle's educational methods that Paul deals with this harder aspect before he comes to speak on the light side of the one revelation. He does not immediately make the whole comfort of the Gospel known as such. This comfort is certainly also present here. But he hides it in the testimony about God's condemnation of man.

The curious 'for' with which 1.18 begins becomes intelligible if we observe that it forms a series with 1.16 and 1.17: 'for it is God's power' and 'for therein is God's righteousness revealed'. The word 'for' in 1.18 is also legitimate. I am not ashamed of the Gospel over against the powers of the metropolis of Rome; because at all events the Gospel as God's almighty work of salvation pronounces God's condemnation of man; because it is more than obvious that I need not be ashamed of the Gospel but that over against the Gospel the Gentile world as concentrated in Rome ought to be ashamed of itself.

That is how Paul first arrives at this subject – almost automatically, still in the course of his introduction. When God and man – the man of the metropolis Rome – meet, as happens in the preaching and hearing of the Gospel, then it is inevitable that the opposition between God and man becomes visible: God's opposition to man's opposition to God. Man's attitude to God is shown up as being one of irreverence – this is the essence of all ungodliness – and of insubordination, of rebellion – this is the essence of all human iniquity. Then there is fire: the fire which consumes the impossible thing man has committed. This fire is God's wrath. God's wrath ought not to be misinterpreted as something foreign and contrary to God's love. But one should understand that God's love is this burning and consuming love. The revelation of God's wrath, of the death-sentence to which God has condemned man because of his sin, is that very act in which God did not spare his own Son but gave him for us all (8.32). The death of Jesus Christ on the cross is the revelation of God's wrath from heaven. That is the starting-point of Paul's argument. It should also be our key to the interpretation of what follows.

Let us admit at once: if 1.19-21[1] had come to us by themselves, say as fragments of an unknown text by an unknown author, then one might possibly conjecture that all these words referred to the existence of a 'natural' knowledge of God by the Gentiles, prior to and independent of God's revelation in Jesus Christ. Time and again these words have been read as though they were such a fragment and they have in fact been interpreted and ever and again quoted as evidence of a general doctrine of such a natural knowledge of God. On that strange

---

[1] For this text Cf. *Kirchliche Dogmatik* (henceforth referred to as *KD*), I, 2, p. 334f. and II, 1, p. 131f. (English translation *Church Dogmatics*, I, 2, p. 306f and II, 1, p. 119ff.)

presupposition too much has even been read into these words. It does not say in these verses, in which the Gentile religions as such are as yet not even mentioned, that the Gentile religions witness to a relationship to God which is indispensable to human existence and that they should be interpreted as the result of God's revelation and man's sin. But even this presupposition is wrong. These verses happen not to be a loose fragment. They occur as the words of the Apostle Paul in a definite context in the Epistle to the Romans and in the whole body of Pauline literature. In view of the conclusion at which the whole section aims, in which they occur, and in view of Paul's corresponding exposition of that hidden wisdom of God, which eye has not seen and ear has not heard, which does not enter into the heart of any man, which the natural man does not accept, which he cannot apprehend, which only the Spirit of God can know and which man can only know through this Spirit of God (I Cor. 2.6-16) – in view of all this it would be very strange indeed, if Paul suddenly regarded the Gentiles as being in full participation and possession of a genuine knowledge of God. If Paul really did reckon with such a possibility, why did he not use it to much better advantage? Why, in the whole remainder of the Epistle to the Romans and in all his other Epistles does he speak about the knowledge of God, as if there were in reality but one knowledge of God, the one which is based on the revelation of that divine verdict and work of salvation and therefore on the revelation in Jesus Christ?

If we consider the text in the light of that context, then it becomes evident at once that Paul is not speaking of the Gentiles as such and in general. He is not speaking in the fashion in which a student of comparative religion or a philosopher of religion would have spoken in his place. Later on he was not to speak of the Jews in that way, either. He is speaking of the Gentiles as they are now confronted with the Gospel, whether they know it or not, and whether they like it or not. They are confronted with the Gospel because of the resurrection of Jesus Christ and because since then the proclamation of his name has been taking its course throughout the world. Paul does something which is done by no student of comparative religion or philosopher of religion: he sees the Gentiles as well as the Jews in the reflected light of that fire of God's wrath which is the fire of his love. He is speaking about something which certainly does concern the Gentiles but which was by no means known to them, which was entirely unknown to them: he tells the Gentiles – and it needs no less than an apostle to tell them this – the greatest news concerning them: that God has in fact for a long time, yea always, since the creation of the world been declaring and revealing himself to them. The world which has always been around them, has always been God's work and as such God's witness to himself. Objectively the Gentiles have always had the opportunity of knowing God, his invisible being, his eternal power and godhead. And again, objectively speaking, they have also always known him. In all that they have known otherwise, God as the Creator of all things has always been, objectively speaking, the proper and real object of their knowledge, exactly in the same sense as undoubtedly the Jews in their Law were objectively dealing with God's revelation.

How does Paul arrive at those statements? We should bear in mind what they are intended to demonstrate: that Gentiles and Jews stand before God without an excuse, fully answerable and responsible for their opposition to him (1.20; 2.1), and that this is visible in the light of God's revelation in Jesus Christ, in the reflected shine of the fire of wrath that was kindled on Golgotha. In that divine accusation and therefore in the revelation in Jesus Christ and therefore in the Gospel – only there and only in that way – Paul sees also that Gentiles and Jews are what they are because they have really come *from* God and are therefore really and seriously in opposition to him and consequently really and seriously subject to God's wrath. They err against their own better knowledge. How can the Gospel be God's almighty power (1.16), if the Gentiles could exculpate themselves by saying that God is a stranger to them, that they are living in some forgotten corner of the world, where God is not God or cannot be known as God – if there were such a thing as a self-contained Gentile world, established, secure and justified in itself, against which God's accusation, wrath and judgment would be unjustified because it could claim that it did not know the Law? But that is exactly what the Gentile world cannot do, what it cannot possibly do, in view of Christ's death on the cross. And that is what Paul in 1.19-21 has proved to be impossible. The Law also applies to those who do not know it, simply because objectively speaking they are subject to it.

Paul does not dream of paying the Gentiles anything resembling a compliment and of trying to find in their religions some point of contact for the understanding of the Gospel; on the contrary he is merely and simply calling them to faith in God's verdict. This is shown by the whole way in which this chapter is continued. In spite of their objective knowledge of God they have not rendered him the honour and the gratitude they owe him. They are in flagrant opposition to the truth about man which has been revealed in Jesus Christ at the same time as the truth about God. Rebelliously they hold that truth down– (1.18). They exchange it for a lie (1.25). Measured by that truth – seen in the light of that truth – their thoughts are vain, empty thoughts, their heart is dark (1.21). Claiming to be wise they have become fools (1.22).

How and to what extent does all that apply? Paul does not reply by first pointing out this or that Gentile vice or aberration. He starts by referring to the best the Gentiles have, or claim to have: their religion, which consists in one great confusion between the Creator and his creatures. If there is any position from which no bridge can possibly be built to the Gospel, to the knowledge of the living God, then this is it! Human religion, as radically distinguished from belief in God's revelation, always originates and consists in this confusion: in the mistaken confidence in which man wants to decide for himself who and what God is, which can only produce this confusion, i.e. idolatry.

That mistaken self-confidence is the actual object of God's

wrath. For it is the essence of man's opposition to God. It is the thing at which God's condemnation of man is aimed and which is in fact affected by it. For everything which Paul now (1.24-31) further mentions in the way of 'natural' and 'unnatural' sins is most emphatically called the result of an 'abandonment' (1.24, 26, 28), which is God's response to the fundamental opposition of man which is his actual sin: the religious sin. He is abandoned and left to himself by God – and that is what makes the Gentile into a Gentile. And the other things follow automatically: all the immorality, for the development of which no large city is needed, but which is also, and perhaps even more, the immorality of the small town, the village and the worthy provinces.

All the allusions in these verses are to be regarded as an illustration, admittedly terrible – but no more than an illustration – of the fundamental thesis that the Gentiles are irreverent and insubordinate, and subject to God's wrath because they suppress the truth, because they exchange it for a lie, because they permit themselves and achieve that confusion between the Creator and the creature. They are subject to God's wrath because – not in their ignorance, but in their wisdom, not in their wickedness but in the best they are capable of, not in the lowest spheres but on the very highest levels of their humanity – they make this effort to seize God's crown. Because they do this all the rest follows by necessity – by necessity because of God's reaction – sin and sins in the popular sense of the word, everything which they know very well for themselves (1.32) is unworthy, yea that it is worthy of death and which all the same they approve and have to approve of in themselves and in others, since they have in practice denied and blasphemed the Creator as Creator.

Note that Paul has avoided using the words 'Gentiles' or 'Greeks' or 'Rome' in this particular context. That he has them in mind follows from the next passage where in contrast and this time emphatically he speaks of the Jews, and from where he looks back on 1.18-32, so that it is obvious that here in fact he has the Gentiles in mind especially. But in the Gentiles he is simply concerned with man as such. When man is confronted with the Gospel, the first thing to be said about him is what is said here. That once more makes it evident that Paul really could not very well be ashamed of the Gospel.

The content of all that follows in 2.1–3.20 can be summed up by saying that the condemnation of man, preached by the Gospel does in fact apply to *all* men. *Everyone* has every reason to apply to himself God's wrath, in the way that it was kindled in the revelation of his very love. Note Paul's own recapitulation and conclusion of the whole argument in 3.9 and 19.

In 2.1 we learn about a man (evidently representing a whole category of men) who wants to put himself forward as an exception. The whole following argument is concerned with him. Note that he is not addressed as a Jew until 2.17. It sounds there as if Paul suddenly gets up, walks towards the window, opens it and speaks out into the street, where opposite the Church of Jesus Christ there is still a synagogue.

But actually it is obvious right from the beginning that Paul means the Jew, who was circumcised, who possesses and reads the books of God's covenant with Abraham, Moses and David, who is the man who has sought and found the realization of his life in the fulfilment of God's Law to the last letter. He regards himself as exculpated from the accusation raised in 1.19ff, as not affected by God's wrath described there. He worships no gods nor idols beside the true God, the Creator of heaven and earth. He could not very well be accused of all the gross sins mentioned in 1.24f; he could not very well be described as one whom God has abandoned to the lusts of his heart, to his 'vile passions' (1.26). He looks upon the life of the Gentile metropolis and the whole Gentile world as a critical spectator who has no part in it, who is really different and superior. It does not occur to him to perceive his own death sentence in the cross of Jesus. On the contrary, represented by the voice of his highest religious authorities and by the voice of the people of Jerusalem he has even brought Jesus to the cross. He has thus demonstrated and declared once more that he will have nothing to do with blasphemy, that blasphemers are excluded from his company, expelled to the Gentiles, into the desert, to die there as they deserve. It is just this kind of Jew, Paul says, who is wrong, who above all others has no excuse.

Evidently the whole problem of the divine condemnation of man through the Gospel becomes completely serious only now, in connection with this, Jewish, man. What after all are those poor Gentiles of 1.19ff with their ungodliness and iniquity compared to the ungodliness and iniquity of this man? What, after all is the pious Gentile, who was examined first so to speak by way of prelude, as compared to the pious Jew, the man of pure religion and morality, not arbitrary but directed by God's own Word? Paul says to just this man: while and because everything that was said in 1.19ff applies to the Gentiles, from the same point of view as it was said of them, it applies – not only to you *too* but to you *in particular*. With you in particular, in your very midst, precisely in what you are and do, this revelation of God's wrath over all ungodliness and iniquity is taking place.

It is precisely 'through the Law', i.e. through the very thing that in fact and quite seriously does distinguish you and mark you out from the evil world of the Gentiles, that there is attained the knowledge, the objective demonstration and identification of sin, which is the object of God's wrath. Thus says the final word of this section (3.20). The only thing is that you do not realize that, just because it is justified – after all you did get it from the Law – the same criticism with which you criticize others, by which you judge and condemn the whole Gentile world, applies to you before it applies to the others, to the Gentile world. For you are the man who does not merely do the same that is done there, *too*. You do it *first* (2.1). We know that the Gentiles, being what they are and doing what they do according to the picture in 1.19ff, are subject to God's judgment, and you are right if you see and say that as well (2.2).

But there is something far more urgent for you to see and to say. For God's judgment takes place 'according to the *truth*'. In 2.5 Paul will say, 'it is God's *just* judgment', and in 7.16 with great emphasis: it takes place 'according to my Gospel, through *Jesus Christ*!' He is the truth, he is the righteousness of God. According to 2.11 that means that God's judgment takes place 'with no respect of persons', which literally means: in such a way that through every mask God sees the real faces of men, so that there is not merely no difference between the Jew who criticizes and the Gentile who is criticized; but the Jew who criticizes even stands in the dock as the man who is first and foremost condemned by God, so that the sins of the Gentiles, the sins of the evil world actually only imitate and illustrate the sins of the Jews. That is as certain as that God's Law has been put in his hands, as certain as that its promises and threats (as twice emphasized very strongly in 2.9, 10) concern him, the Jew first, and only then indirectly the Gentile. As Jesus Christ is the Judge, all men (but – how could it be otherwise – first the Jews among whom he arose) are responsible for their relationship to that Law according to which *he* judges, which *he* carries out, and they are therefore responsible for their relationship to *him*. The Jews critically keep a distance from that which the Gentiles according to 1.19ff are and do. This is certainly very proper, but by it the Jew cannot hope himself to escape from God's judgment, which is the judgment of Jesus Christ: for he himself first and foremost does the same as the Gentiles (2.3). For it is – and he should not overlook, nor despise this – the 'wealth of God's kindness, forbearance and patience', it is God's grace towards man that is in action in his true and righteous judgment through Jesus Christ (2.4). Paul is not speaking of just any condemnation of man, but of his condemnation through the Gospel, through the good news that announces and warrants his salvation, the good news, that he may die as the old ungodly and iniquitous man which he is, yea that as such he has already died in Jesus Christ, in his death at Golgotha, and that he may now live an entirely different and new life, in Jesus Christ, risen from the dead. This condem-

c

33

nation of man leads and drives him to repentance, to a renewal of his thinking and being. That is how it affects him, the Jew, first. That is how it puts him first under the wrath of God. And on this (not 'for this') wonderfully salutary day of the wrath and the revelation of God's righteous judgment, the Jew – he evidently fails to recognize, he despises the merciful meaning of this day, the day of Jesus Christ – cannot think of anything better to do but to 'treasure up wrath' for himself. He is content with seeing and saying how badly the Gentiles are behaving and how very different he appears as compared to them (2.5).

But God's wrath, God's judgment that man must die in order to live is, of course, not meant for disinterested contemplation, neither as far as it concerns the Gentiles, nor as far as it concerns the Jews. And those who store it up with others in mind, store it up for themselves. Those who, as far as others are concerned, stop at the death-sentence, seal their own death-sentence. God's judgment is to be heard to the end, exactly as it stands: that we shall die so that we may *live* – as the judgment of God's kindness, forbearance and patience over all human ungodliness and iniquity. The Jew does not want to hear it to the end, at least not as far as others are concerned. Thus he reveals the stubbornness and impenitence of his heart in the face of the judgment, and remains under it as his death-sentence. Because (2.6) 'God renders to everyone according to his works'. Before the judgment-seat of Jesus Christ we receive exactly what is due to us according to whether, in what we are and do, we are prepared to hear his judgment right to the end, or not. If we do, we may then also take its beginning – that as sinners we are subject to God's wrath and must die – absolutely seriously and therefore repent sincerely with that blessed end in view. In our decision concerning God's revealed grace we stand or fall according to whether we allow it to be grace, God's unmerited favour towards others and towards ourselves – or not. By his criticism of the Gentiles the Jew proves that he will not allow it to be grace and therefore he will be put to shame

34

first of all. That is his failure to appreciate God, his insubordination, compared to which all the idolatry and immorality of the pious and impious Gentiles is really no more than a weakly reflected image.

What it means for God to render to everyone according to his works, is developed in 2.7-10 in the light of the statement of 2.11. In view of that criterion of God's no mask will do – and that whole alleged special position of the Jews is a mask. For God (2.16), when judging the works of men, searches their hearts. 2.7-10 are a variation of the same thought: the Jew first and then also the Greek is exposed to God's wrath, to God's judgment that man is worthy of death inasmuch as he chooses and does the evil work of impenitence, inasmuch as he does not choose and do the good work of penitence (1.32). For according to the whole context and to the wording the real issue is that it is essential to become obedient to the truth instead of to iniquity (2.8). It is therefore essential to accept God's grace in his judgment and consequently to submit to his judgment and to repent. It is essential to persist in *this* good work as the proper way to glory, to honour and to incorruption (2.7). The faithfulness of faith, which recognizes and accepts in God's righteous judgment the word of his mercy, is essential. Those who did that work would really receive glory, honour and peace (2.10). But those who do not want to do that work, who exhibit that contentiousness (perhaps the attitude of the paid labourer) which is characteristic of the Jews' attitude to the Gentiles, and in that contentiousness the impenitence which desires no grace and which therefore cannot humble itself, what can they expect from this seat of judgment but wrath and anger, trouble and anguish (2.8)? By appearing before this judgment seat in this frame of mind he has already chosen that, he has already condemned himself.

Why does it not help the Jew to claim that he, and only he, has, knows and keeps God's Law? According to 2.12-16 it does not help him, because God – the God who now pronounces his judgment on man in Jesus Christ – searches the hearts.

35

Consequently those who have the Law and those who do not have it are confronted with the same question: are they doing or are they not doing what the Law demands? If they are not, then they perish with the Law just as well as without it (2.12). In the judgment of Jesus Christ the issue is not whether men are hearers, but whether they are doers of the Law (2.13). And there are in fact (2.14, 15) doers of the Law who are its hearers but not at all in the sense in which the Jews are. For there are people, who, in miraculous fulfilment of Jer. 31.33 have his Law put in their inward parts and written in their hearts, people to whom, in fulfilment of Ezek. 11.19; 36.26 he has given a new heart so that they are now a law unto themselves and in their human nature, without having the Law, do what the Law demands. Their conscience is the place where the prohibitions and commandments of the Law stand opposite each other in the form of their own thoughts, though they do not have the Law, though they are Gentiles by nature. In 2.26ff Paul was again to refer to those remarkable doers of the Law, who after all have not heard it in the same way as the Jews: those circumcised without circumcision.

In view of that other passage in this chapter, and also in view of the prophecies evidently referred to, it is very foolish to think, as has been thought, that in 2.14-15 Paul was speaking of just any Gentiles who did in fact fulfil the Law because of some moral law of nature written in their hearts. That would obviously be just as little in keeping with what is said in 1.19-32 about what the Gentiles are and do, or with 3.9, 19, as was the application of 1.19-21 to a natural knowledge of God of the Gentiles.

The Gentiles whom in 2.14-15 Paul mentions in contrast to the Jews are simply the Gentile *Christians* (Paul addresses them in the same short style, e.g. in 11.13; 15.9), to whom, through God's wonderful deed in Jesus Christ, the very thing has happened which those prophetic words promised to the people of Israel. To them God has given his Holy Spirit and therefore a new heart that recognizes God's will in such a manner that they can now do it and carry it out. Consequently – admittedly a tremendous revolution – they now stand in contrast to the Israelites. For as the latter have not been guided in the same way, they are still gathered in the obstinate Synagogue, as a confirmation of their accusation. In the Synagogue particularly God's will is read but not done; because the good work of penitence is left undone, there grace is not left to be grace but defamed.

And, as is shown in 2.17-24, it does not profit the Jew that no doubt he makes an effort to keep the written Law, the Ten Commandments, and that (as described in detail in 2.17-20) in theory and in practice he undoubtedly does adopt a 'moral-ethical' standpoint and unequivocally shows it to be such. Though there may be some irony in these words, they are not merely ironical, but also a sincere acknowledgement of the position and the mission which the Jews have in fact been given in the Gentile metropolis and in the whole Gentile world. For according to so many passages in the OT Israel is as it is regarded here: 'a guide of the blind, a light to those who are in the dark, a teacher of the simple.' In its Law it really does possess 'the embodiment (the form) of knowledge and truth'. But only their form, and, in spite of all endeavours to live according to that form, not knowledge and truth themselves. For Jesus Christ is knowledge and truth, the essence and the sum total of the Law (10.4). In their relationship to him the Jews not only fail to do the Law (2.12-16), but they transgress (2.23), they break every one of the Ten Commandments, they fail to fulfil Israel's lofty function in the world, they do not render honour to God but cause him – this was prophesied about them in Ezek. 36.20 – dishonour among the Gentiles. Though the picture of 2.21-22 is to be taken literally it should not be regarded as a portrayal of particular atrocities or bad habits for which Paul wants to blame contemporary Jewry. The Jews are thieves, adulterers, desecrators by what they did to Jesus Christ on the day of Golgotha and which, in spite of his resurrection they continue to do by declining to accept the glad message of the grace which has appeared in him, and by persecuting the Church which praises that grace. Who delivered his Messiah to the Gentiles and with him his God? And who does that again and again? The fact that the Jew has made and still makes himself guilty of that, deprives him – and him first of all, as we notice here in particular – of the opportunity of having any honour before God which might free him from the accusation that concerns all men.

And therefore even circumcision (2.25-29) and his separation from the Gentiles of which it is a physical sign is of no avail to the Jew. For circumcision is related to the Law. It marks the setting apart for the keeping of the Law. But if the Law is not kept – and as demonstrated it is in fact not kept by the Jews, but broken – then that setting apart is *de facto* abrogated, then they – and they first of all – are in the same position as the Gentiles. They are then ungodly and iniquitous and under God's wrath, and no circumcision can alter this (2.25). Once more the Jews are actually put to shame by the existence of uncircumcised people who by repenting and believing keep and fulfil the requirements of the Law, and whose uncircumcision is therefore counted to them for circumcision, so that in God's sight and therefore in reality they participate in Israel and in all the promises of Israel (2.26). The existence of those who are uncircumcised by nature (once more Paul is referring to the Gentile Christians) now repeats the verdict on the circumcised, who are manifestly circumcised only externally, according to the letter (2.27).

For who is actually – in God's sight and therefore in reality – a Jew, a child of Abraham, a member of the people of Moses, an heir to the promises made to David? Surely not the man who is one according to race and blood, because of the circumcision performed on his body, in short not the man who is circumcised 'outwardly' in the eyes and the opinions of men (2.28), but the one who is circumcised in the secret places of his heart, which are open to God and where God judges and distinguishes between clean and unclean, between those who

38

are his people and those who are not. That Jew would be praiseworthy as a Jew who, in those secret places, would be found praiseworthy and would in fact be praised not by man's judgment but by God's (2.29). But he would be a Christian – no matter whether from among the Jews or from among the Gentiles. He would be a Christian, who praises God's grace and therefore accepts his judgment, who is therefore not trying to escape from the divine condemnation. He does not try to save himself from it but surrenders to it in order that he may glory in the mercy of him who condemns him to death. The Jew who tries to exculpate himself because he regards himself as an exception does not do so, and that is precisely why he is not praised and why he is and remains wholly without excuse (2.1).

In the next passage, 3.1-8, we are dealing with a series of statements – more or less interruptions which could have been made here, and which probably were in fact all made in Paul's day. They are tackled, together with Paul's brief answers, but it is hardly possible to discover any proper order of thought until the argument is resumed in 3.9.

3.1-2: Do Judaism and circumcision then have no value at all; do they have no real and permanent distinction? Paul replies that to think that would be the greatest possible mistake. The Jews are and remain the nation entrusted with the words, the revelations of God up to and including the person of Jesus Christ. The Gentiles, when they attain to faith, can in a way only be their guests. It must rest at this: 'Salvation comes from the Jews' (John 4.22).

3.3-4: Does not the fact that some Jews (there are very many) do not believe, imply an abrogation of God's faithfulness? Why has this faithful God not simply made all the members of his people into faithful members? Paul replies that God's faithfulness cannot be abrogated. But it is the faithfulness of his truth, i.e. of his revelation. As regards this, every man, as such, is blind, or rather, actively, a liar. God has therefore no obligations to anybody. He is not tied to anyone, not even to the members of his people. If in that nation there is opposition to him, apostasy from him, then this goes to demonstrate even more powerfully that it is solely due to his grace that there are any faithful at all, that in his judgment – for this is the only thing that matters – he remains true to himself, inasmuch as those who have been justified by his mercy, can ever only glory in that mercy (Paul returned to those two questions more extensively in Chapters 9-11).

3.5-6: But if 3.3-4 are right after all, why, and with what right is God angry with those who do not render to him the obedience of faith? Paul answers: God is and remains the Judge of the world, although and because he makes even the iniquity of men serve the purpose of the showing forth of his righteousness as such, his faithfulness to himself and consequently his grace. If he kills to bring to *life*, then this can only mean that he *kills* to bring to life. Who would dare, and who could appeal *to* God *against* God?

3.7-8 are a more pointed repetition of the same question. So the truth, the revelation of God is exalted, is triumphant by the very means of the human lie, from which it is distinguished so clearly by the justification of believers? Paul did in fact write in 5.20: 'Where sin became great, there grace itself became exceedingly great.' Does my lie therefore serve that becoming exceedingly great, that brilliant light of grace, and consequently the glory of God? Why must I then be exposed to the judgment? Are not right they, are they not consistent who draw the conclusion: 'let us do evil that good may come of it?' Here particularly Paul's reply is as short as the question is long. 'Their damnation (the damnation of those who argue like that) is justly due' (RV: 'Whose condemnation is just'). Why is he so brief? Because fools, and consistent fools in particular can and should be answered briefly. And in that long question everything is foolish, everything is wrong. The things which Paul in this whole section has called evil: impenitence, the rejection of Jesus Christ, unbelief, can obviously not be committed so that good may come of them and grace consequently be triumphant! And conversely, those who desire the triumph of grace will not lie, but repent and so be obedient to the truth. What God wants to do with the lie and the liar is his business. But we have been called by God not to lie, but to render honour to the truth and so to him.

And finally there is the summary in 3.9-20: No one has any advantage in the face of God's judgment. Jews and Gentiles, men as such are all under the dominion of sin, i.e. under that dominion under which they are and must remain the object of God's wrath. That is the view of the Old Testament which is in the hands of these very Jews. In 3.11-18 there is in a long series of OT quotations.

For a proper understanding of all these sayings we should remember that Paul does not hear them as spoken by some prophet or psalmist but by Jesus Christ as the One to whom the OT witnesses and who witnesses to himself in the OT through the voice of the fathers. He is the Judge. His Law is the Law of which 3.19 says that it speaks to all who are under the Law, i.e. all whom it addresses, whom it encounters. And in the Gospel it confronts the whole world and therefore every mouth is stopped and the whole world is declared guilty before God by the Law, or rather by the Judge who applies and executes the Law. Before God's Law as such and in itself, all flesh, all mankind is without justification, in spite of all their works (3.20). To be justified with its works before God and his Law mankind would have to be a different mankind, radically renewed. In Chapter 2 (vv. 14-15 and 26-29) Paul has already hinted that there is such a new mankind and where it can be found. But apart from that possibility, or rather from that new reality (3.21ff) he must leave it at this: what follows from the Law, and from the Gospel itself inasmuch as it is God's Law, is the knowledge of sin (3.20): the revelation of God's condemnation of man, to which as such we must submit for our salvation, to which we are allowed to submit to our rich comfort.

The Gospel as the Divine Justification of those who believe

FOR our salvation we are allowed and for our rich consolation we are bidden to submit to the divine condemnation. For it is the Gospel which reveals to us this wrath of God. This wrath of God is only the hard, bitter shell in which we have to receive God's judgment – in which we are really permitted to receive God's judgment! For to those who do accept it, it is the omnipotent work of their salvation (1.16). Why that divine condemnation of man in 1.18–3.20, that accusation against each and everyone (3.9), that stopping of every mouth, that exposure of sin by the application of God's Law (3.20)? What does Jesus the Judge want when this happens without exception, to Jews and Greeks before his judgment seat? And what was Paul leading up to, when in the first part of this Epistle he reminded them of that judgment? We shall now learn that, especially in this message, the issue is not the rejection of men, but their salvation, their welfare and beatitude. To receive these we are standing before this Judge, and Paul has reminded us of the judgment of this Judge in order to invite and urge us to receive them with gladness.

But how? Have men not deserved their rejection? Has their condemnation not taken place? Is there anything to be expected but the execution of God's wrath by their punishment? Will Paul be able to speak of anything but death and hell (1.32)? Or was the condemnation perhaps not meant quite seriously? Has God after all let himself be persuaded, has God out of some capricious kindness allowed himself to be bargained with?

Does God's love consist in this: that his wrath is after all not quite so dangerous as it may appear at first, that in reality he can also act otherwise? Is it the secret of the Gospel, the soft centre in the hard shell that perhaps things are not so bad, that God can also act otherwise?

But the continuation of the Epistle neither says that men are deservedly consumed and destroyed by God's wrath, nor does it speak of this kind of love and kindness of God, which would in its weakness be very suspect. Rather, it continues to speak further, and more than ever, of God's judgment. We must note that it does not speak of a suspension, nor of an amnesty, nor of an indulgence, but of God's judgment, as it has actually taken place and as it is proclaimed in its entirety, and as man may also hear and understand it if only he accepts it and applies it to himself, if only he does not regard himself as an exception to whom it does not apply. For as all those can hear who hear it in its entirety and apply it entirely to themselves – for everyone who believes, Paul has already said in 1.17, and he will now say it again – its verdict is that man is neither damned, nor merely granted an amnesty, he is acquitted by God, declared innocent and therefore justified. And because he has been justified, 5.1ff will demonstrate, therefore and therein he is also placed in a position of peace with God. But first of all it must be understood that he has been justified in God's severe and true judgment which searches the hearts and is no respecter of persons.

All that long and harsh section 1.18–3.20 is nothing but one explanation of the fact that you are the man – i.e. the man to whom God's verdict applies and who admits that it applies to him. He who accepts it, saying, 'Yes, I am that man!', shall hear this: 'You are the man whom God has justified!' And again he shall answer: 'Yes, I am this man! this man I am allowed to be and I desire to be.' That is the good centre in the hard shell; it is the subject of the section 3.21–4.25. It shows that the Gospel is the divine justification of those who believe.

The beginning of 3.21 immediately reminds us of 1.17:

God's righteousness has been made manifest. But the Greek expression used here by Paul is different, more specified, meaning not so much that something which has so far been hidden, is unveiled, as that it becomes visible. And then, as distinguished from 1.17, Paul also adds: 'without (literally "outside") the Law'. And he starts by saying 'but now'. This 'but now' contrasts the revelation described in 1.18–3.20 to the mistaken opinion which, after that description, might arise from a mistaken Jewish or Gentile way of thinking, as if the only possibilities left were either our damnation or a weak clemency on God's part. But no, God's just verdict itself has now been revealed as an act of his righteousness which does not mean our damnation. Note how in 3.25-26 Paul holds on to this and how the notion of righteousness dominates the end of Chapter 3 and the whole of Chapter 4. The point at issue is the demonstration of God's *righteousness*, but that means its *demonstration*, i.e. the manifestation of the entire contents of his judgment by which those mistaken opinions are put right from the beginning.

The words 'without the Law' primarily define an empty space. Their positive meaning can only be made clear by what follows. Of one thing we can be quite sure in view of 3.31, they cannot mean that the Law is abrogated, shattered, invalidated. Paul says there that, more than by anything else, the Law is put into full force and motion by what we now have to say of God's verdict, in view of his revelation. But to understand that verdict we must not – and that is the meaning of the words 'without the Law' – direct our attention to the Law. That is, we must neither direct our attention to what God wants and demands of man, nor to that which we do and by which we all (according to 1.18–3.20) do *not* fulfil the Law. What the Gospel, in agreement with Moses and the prophets has to say about the Law (and also about our inevitable condemnation) that we must understand as a *testimony* by which (as in 1.18–3.20) we are guided and prepared, for the heart of the matter, by which we are summoned to listen to the full content of that verdict.

What actually is that full content? It is (3.22) the judgment which was revealed and which has become effective through faith in *Jesus Christ*, i.e. through the message concerning that faith, and for the faith in that message, and which thus comes to everyone who believes. To understand that verdict we have to direct our attention to him and not to what God wants and demands of us or to that which we do and which is so entirely contrary to his demands. We must direct our attention to the Judge himself. Were we to neglect him, to direct our attention somewhere else, then we should only discover (3.23) what according to 1.18–3.20 is certainly an undeniable reality: 'There is no distinction, for all have sinned and fall short of glory before God (of the glory of God, RV).'

But we ought not to neglect him, we ought not to direct our attention to the Law. If we did this we would still not accept God's judgment exactly as it is nor apply it to ourselves as coming from him and in the sense in which it is meant. Should we want to direct our attention to the Law, we would, according to 1.18–3.20, have to be asked once more if we have not yet understood that we are condemned, that we are not at all in a position to look the Law in the face and to measure ourselves by it. But instead of that, 'without the Law' we must and may look upon the Judge and hear from his lips that those who, according to the Law proclaimed and applied by him, are sinners and have no glory before God (3.24), have been justified because they cleave to him, because they believe in him. That however is purely a gift. It is not their merit – where could they have earned it? – but God's grace, the free work of divine kindness and favour which they have in no way provoked, on which they have no claim whatsoever.

Is God therefore lying, when he justifies them, when he declares them to be what they are not? No, but in that very word of grace he speaks the truth and exercises the strictest justice. For they are justified because they have been delivered in Jesus Christ, i.e. because he has redeemed them from the whole dominion of sin under which they are because of the Law and from the whole curse which according to the Law should therefore fall upon them: as slaves whose freedom has been paid for and on whom their former master therefore has no more claim. What has happened? By shedding his blood as a man, and giving up his life, the Judge himself, before whom they have all been called to account, before whom they are all transgressors and lost, has (3.25) become the propitiatory sacrifice for the entire people of those who believe in him. He has shouldered the responsibility for the punishment which must needs follow their condemnation, and for all the effects of God's wrath. This has already taken effect in his death. God's forbearance towards the iniquity and ungodliness of men has reached its end and aim in his death. In his death God has made the necessary angry end with the sinners. And so the guilt – not his guilt, but the guilt of his people, in whose place he has sacrificed himself – has been disposed of, so that there is now not one unjust person left among his people. Those who are his people – i.e. all those who believe on him – are righteous, innocent, clean. For in the death of the Judge Jesus Christ before whom they stand and whose judgment they accept, an effective end has been made of their iniquity and ungodliness, of themselves as sinners. That they are his people and may accept his judgment in faith in him, is a gift, that is grace. But that God justifies them, that is a word of purest truth, that is an act of his strictest righteousness.

It is as if Paul could hardly emphasize enough (3.26) that in that which the Gospel has to say to the present generation – as the foundation of an entirely new, unique present – the real issue is the demonstration, the manifestation of God's *righteousness*. God is *righteous* when he justifies him who meets him 'with the faith' in Jesus, whom 'faith' in the Judge who was judged for him has led to the admission: I am the man! The whole Epistle to the Romans is concerned with repeating, interpreting and explaining the knowledge expressed in 3.21-26 that our relationship to God is one of law, regulated by Jesus Christ. In the faith in Jesus Christ we have been given that legitimate ground of our existence before God. Thus we have

46

been given everything, really everything. That is what Paul calls the Gospel.

What follows in the remainder of this section, 3.21–4.25, has a double intention. Paul wants to make it clear that, and to what extent, the manifestation of the divine verdict as the justification of all believers is not a new revelation, but (3.21) has been witnessed 'by the Law and the prophets', i.e. by the OT, and is consequently merely the confirmation of the truth of the OT. And in the course of that explanation he wants to make a point of setting forth what that faith in Jesus Christ is all about, in which that divine verdict is manifested.

3.27-31 are a short series of disconnected interruptions similar to 3.1-9. Paul then stops at the question raised in 4.1, to devote the remaining larger part of this section to it.

3.27a: What room is there left for boasting, i.e. the boasting of a man who might regard himself as unaffected by the divine verdict? The reply is that it is out of the question. Because man's honour has been legitimately restored in Jesus Christ, it is now definite (3.23) that man by himself, apart from Jesus Christ, has no honour and therefore nothing of which he can boast before God.

3.27b-28: By what law, by which norm is man measured when these hard words are applied to him? By the measure of his works, by that which he does or fails to do? The answer is no, for according to that law some honour might perhaps be due to him, as well as much dishonour. To men such as Abraham even much honour might be due. But man has no reason to boast because he is measured by the law of faith, by the fact that our legitimate claim is the Judge who was condemned for us. That he is justified as a believer excludes the possibility of his being justified by his works, by himself. To the extent that he would want himself to satisfy the Law and to justify himself in this way he would be neglecting Jesus Christ, he would not believe and therefore not be justified. When Luther in 3.28 added the word 'alone' to the words 'by faith' he underlined exactly what Paul did in fact say without that word.

47

3.29-30: Or might God – the God who justifies man – be the God of the Jews but the God of the Jews only and not of the Gentiles too? Would the only people to be righteous before him be found in the particular sphere of his chosen people? The answer is that he is the God of the Jews *and* of the Gentiles. In the very regulation of the relationship between himself and man through Jesus Christ and faith in him God proves himself as *one God*. All monotheism is cold and idle talk as long as God has not been recognized as the One who has pronounced this verdict. But as such he is no further from the Gentiles than from the Jews. And as regards them the Jews ought not to try to go back to an honour which would allow them to neglect Jesus Christ.

3.31: Does all this not mean the abrogation of the Law? If we must not look there for an answer to the question of our righteousness before God, what are we to think of all that God desires and demands of us, as we can read on every page of the OT. The answer is: 'impossible' (the Greek is an expression which Paul always uses as a sign of extreme horror). Paul is not dreaming of an abrogation of the Law. On the contrary: 'we establish the Law!' We teach men to understand the Law; how on every page of the OT it desires and demands just this; that we must believe in God's promise – that we must believe in the promise of God that has now been fulfilled in Jesus Christ. For we preach the *obedience* of faith (1.5) and therefore certainly no lawlessness but the validity of the Law. For Jesus Christ is the sum total and the fulfilment of the Law (10.4) because he has fulfilled and satisfied it, because he has left to the genuine hearer of the Law only that truly active obedience which consists in faith: faith in him, the Judge who was condemned for us and through whom only we are righteous before God – but therefore really and fully righteous.

It is obvious that all these questions as well as those in 3.1-9 are somehow connected with the problem of the proper interpretation of the Old Testament. Paul must often have heard these questions from Jewish, Jewish-Christian but certainly also from Gentile Christian readers of the Holy Scriptures. He stops at the last of them (4.1) and devotes the whole fourth chapter to it. The question is certainly sufficiently radical and comprehensive to merit that distinction. For it is this: 'What shall we then say that Abraham our forefather according to the flesh hath found?'

According to the view, certainly correct, of the contemporary readers of the OT Abraham was *the* righteous man, the proto-type of all the other faithful. By calling him 'our forefather according to the flesh' Paul acknowledges that he himself is a Jew and places himself among the first to inquire about the proper interpretation of the OT. The question in 4.1 means: What then made Abraham a righteous man?

The reply is given in three parts: 4.2-8, 9-12 and 13-17a. Here three mistaken answers are rejected and at the same time the correct answer is supplied, that faith made Abraham a righteous man; and a final part 4.17b-22 in which an exposition is given of the nature and character of Abraham's faith. In 4.22-25 Paul draws the conclusions and resumes the thread of the argument which he had left in 3.26.

Paul says in 4.2-8 that Abraham is righteous through his faith *and not through his works*. Certainly Abraham can also show works, praiseworthy works. The reader of the OT re-members how he left his native country, he remembers the sacrifice of Isaac. But if such works are Abraham's glory in the eyes of the reader according to the Scriptures, his glory before God is something else. For the Scriptures say that this was counted unto him for righteousness: that he believed God. 'Counted for righteousness', i.e. accepted as righteousness, though that which is accepted in itself, as Abraham's action, has nothing to do with righteousness. Or rather, it is only con-cerned with righteousness to the extent that it is Abraham's relationship to a legitimate claim which he himself cannot pro-vide, which as such is beyond him, which must be given to him, so that his faith can be counted unto him for righteousness because of the righteousness of the objective basis on which the faith rests. Had Abraham been justified by his works the Scriptures would have given an entirely different account: they would have said that the good which he had done had, duly and justly, according to his merits, been counted as his accomplishments for the achievement of righteousness. But now, when speaking of his righteousness, the Scriptures neglect everything that he has done and that has distinguished him from the ungodly. They only have attention for his faith, in which he stands before God as ungodly and yet justified. Similarly in Ps. 32.1f the man is called blessed whom God treats in such a way as though there were nothing to say about him except that he needs the forgiveness of sin. Only that man who calls himself blessed solely because of what he receives as a lost sinner – that God from his side has a legitimate reason to forgive him, to justify him and therefore to treat him as righteous – only that man, i.e. only the believer is righteous before God, as it is written concerning Abraham.

In 4.9-12 Paul says that Abraham is righteous through his faith and *not because of his circumcision*. Abraham is the first bearer of the sign which distinguishes the people of Israel from other nations as God's chosen people. Is righteousness before God tied to that sign and therefore limited to its bearers and therefore to Israel? Does that saying concerning Abraham's righteousness, does Ps. 32.1 (as was already asked in 3.29) only apply to the Jews? The answer of Scripture itself is that it was not Abraham's circumcision but his faith that was counted unto him for righteousness. Conversely, the circumcision was the sign which was to confirm this righteousness of Abraham's which consisted in his faith alone. For he believed while he was as yet uncircumcised, and of this faith before his circumcision it is said that it was counted unto him for righteousness. As one who was *circumcised*, as a Jew, he was the father of the Jews, the nation that was destined to be the bearer of the promise and eventually to receive in the midst of it the fulfilment of the promise, the nation which by this sign was distinguished from other nations for the sake of this promise. But at the same time, as someone as yet uncircumcised, Abraham was the father and forerunner of all those who also as such, as non-Jews, believe in the promise with him and just like him and in that belief would be righteous before God. Circumcision as the mark of the people of the promise can do no more than point to this righteousness before God. Circumcision justifies no one. There are, as Abraham himself proves, people who are righteous before God without circumcision, without Judaism, but not without faith.

In 4.13-17*a* Paul says that Abraham is righteous through his faith and *not as one who knows the Law*. Certainly Abraham's people are the nation to which God's Law was given, to which God's will and command were made known. But that is not what makes Israel the chosen people, the people of the promise. Having and knowing the Law is no participation in the blessing which God has promised for the future. For though it was given and though it is known, the Law has caused Israel nothing but disgrace. Again and again belief in one's own fulfilment of the Law has proved to be a vain belief and the promise as an end to be reached by human effort and action has again and again proved a vain promise. As was shown in 1.18–3.20, the Law as such and by itself is the instrument of God's wrath. 'But where there is *no* Law, *there* is no transgression!' In Israel, too, freedom from sin, righteousness can only be found 'without the Law', i.e. not because of its fulfilment by men (which was never achieved!) but as the righteousness of those people who recognized and seized in the Law God's objective and legitimate reason to forgive their sins. Those in Israel who believed rightly, who did not believe an imaginary promise but the promise which was fulfilled at the end of the history of Israel, they have believed in God himself and in his grace. All those who have done this are Abraham's children, within and without the reach of the Law – who have believed with Abraham, the many nations whose father he has been as the precursor in the faith.

The last phrase gives Paul occasion to enter into a positive description of Abraham's faith: 4.17*b*-18. How does Abraham believe? How, thus, is he a righteous man? In 4.17*b* we are told: he believes in the God who makes the dead live and calls that which is not into being. He therefore believes in the God who is both the Creator of the world, incomprehensible to us, in which there is no death, and also the incomprehensible Creator of the present world, who by his word alone creates something radically new. Faith consists in clinging to the word of this God. In this way Abraham believed. According to the Scriptures this faith was counted unto him for righteousness. In 4.18 we learn that contrary to all expectation, i.e. all the expectation that is humanly possible, he had to expect the fulfilment of what God had promised him. Without the support of any humanly evident reality he had to accept that in God's word he had been given hope. That he did. That was his faith that was counted unto him for righteousness. In 4.19-20 we learn that Abraham was confronted with nothing but natural facts which contradicted his faith. When he received the promise he saw nothing but his own old age and that of his wife Sarah. He did not however pay any attention to this fact. He made no comparison between what he saw and what he heard as God's word. He refrained from any calculation concerning the possibility of its fulfilment and only listened to what he was told. He did not view his existence before God's word with doubt, i.e. from both a 'believing' and a 'worldly' point of view – this dualism is the essence of doubt. He judged from the one point of view which one might think cannot be a point of view at all. He did not treat unbelief as a second possibility, only as an impossibility which was out of the question. All this was the strength of his faith that was counted to him as righteousness. Not for its own sake, not because of the beauty and the depth of his faith! But because by it he gave glory to God (4.20), i.e. because in everything he directed his attention away from himself to God, to let him be God, as the One who has the power, the omnipotence to do, to fulfil what he has promised and from whose faithfulness such fulfilment may be expected under any circumstances. Because Abraham's faith was this directing of his attention from himself to God, it was counted unto him for righteousness (4.22).

So this is Abraham, the righteous man of the OT. He cannot be appealed to as a witness against the Gospel. He and the whole OT can only be appealed to as a witness for the Gospel, as a witness of the divine justification of those who believe.

4.23-25 conclude the series of interruptions which started in 3.27. We remember that the whole statement on Abraham, which dominates the fourth chapter, was merely an extensive reply to the last of the questions raised in 3.27–4.1. That last question had been: 'What makes Abraham the just man which, according to the OT, he was? The answer was not his works, nor his circumcision, nor the Law, but only the fact that he believed, i.e. that he trusted God's word of promise spoken to him, and that he therefore trusted God's almighty power, faithfulness and constancy. Because he gave God the glory, God himself became his righteousness, and he himself, who was ungodly, was acquitted and justified by God (4.5)! Such was Abraham's righteousness. And if we think once more of the whole series of questions raised in 3.27ff we perceive that Paul means that the same is true of everything which in the OT is called the righteousness of man. The Old Testament (3.21) witnesses to *this* righteousness: the righteousness of faith. But what was written of Abraham – 4.23 now resumes the argument – was written of *us*, who now, today, by believing in Jesus Christ, may rejoice in God's verdict revealed in Jesus Christ as our acquittal, as our justification in the judgment. Who was it but Jesus Christ in whom even Abraham trusted and believed when he trusted God's promise? For, indeed, Jesus Christ was the seed promised to Abraham in Isaac! In that way, and therefore in him, Abraham gave glory to the almighty power, faithfulness and constancy of God. In that way, and therefore in him, God himself was Abraham's right-

53

eousness. We believe no differently from Abraham, and in none other than Abraham did and all the other faithful of the OT with him. For we simply believe in the fulfilment, of the promise given to him which has now taken place. And therefore we know with him, but more so, that our righteousness, the righteousness of every man before God can only consist in faith, only in the fact that our faith is counted unto us for righteousness – we repeat: not because of its strength, quality and beauty, but only because of its object, because of Jesus Christ, because of the omnipotence, fidelity and constancy of God, continued, revealed and active in him.

This is once more confirmed, with reference to 3.22-26 in a brief passage, 4.24-25. We are righteous before God because God counts to us our faith for righteousness, as he once did to Abraham. God does this because he, on whom we believe is the God who raised Jesus from the dead as our Lord, i.e. who in the exaltation of this Man, in the revelation of the life of his own Son in this murdered son of man, has made himself our Lord and Head (1.5). He has appointed and delivered him, his own Son (and in him himself *for us*), to do away with, completely to eliminate and make good all our transgressions, so that in his death they have been done away with and cannot disturb us any more. And he has raised this son of David (and in him us *through himself*) from the death which we had deserved, to which we were subject. He has raised him to be our Lord and Head under whom we may exist as people, who – as their old evil garment has been taken off for ever – are now clothed with his righteousness, the righteousness of his Son which is his own righteousness. If we cleave to him as our Lord, if we trust that he is our Head, then we stand before God exactly as his beloved Son does, then he sees us in him and therefore in his own image, then he can find nothing about us but his own righteousness. When we believe in this God of Abraham the righteousness of this God is counted unto us for our own, then it is our righteousness as well as his, then we are, with Abraham, truly and legitimately righteous before him.

The Gospel as Man's Reconciliation with God

ACCORDING to what the Epistle to the Romans has so far told us, God's verdict, made and revealed in Jesus Christ, is contained and hidden in the condemnation of all men (1.18–3.20) which is the justification of those who believe (3.21–4.25). This verdict of God is the Gospel. But in 1.16 Paul also said something else about the Gospel. He said the decisive thing about its contents and scope, i.e. that it is God's almighty *work of salvation* to everyone who believes. We have already noticed that this is not a second thing added to a first to the divine verdict. On the contrary, it is identical with the latter: we have been saved because as believers we have been justified. Conversely: by being justified as believers we have been saved, as is plainly stated in 5.1 regarding the fundamental fact of man's reconciliation with God.

But the fact that this identity does exist must and will now be shown in a series of four closely related arguments in Chapters 5-8: we receive the salvation which as men we need when we hear and accept God's verdict in faith. That verdict is therefore no empty word. Being God's verdict, it has the irresistible power of the truth which Paul has already attributed to it in 1.16: he who is righteous before God can just for that reason not be lost. The man on whom God looks and whom God judges as he looks on his own beloved Son, as he looks on himself in this mirror, is therefore safe and exalted with God. And therefore his prospects during the short time of his existence here and now cannot be bad but only good. As was already stated in 1.17 he must and shall *live*. The righteous man, who

55

through his faith is righteous before God, will by and through that faith not die in God's presence but live. He will live in the covenant with God and he will therefore not have an anxious, clouded, desperate life, but (5.17) a royal, a sovereign life, that eternal life that the ever-living God has granted him as his partner in the covenant.

The first of many things which must be said about this is the assertion in 5.1 that as believers who are for that reason righteous we are men who have been reconciled with God. In this reconciliation God's saving hand, so to speak, grips us. We must observe that neither here nor anywhere else in the NT is there any question of God being reconciled to us, but only of our being reconciled to him. God does not need to be reconciled. For God loves even when he is angry. Moreover, God has not cast the burden of his wrath on us so that we should have to be set free from it. By making his own Son suffer and die he has taken it on to himself, so that it cannot touch and destroy us. God's righteousness needs no mitigation, as if he could only be reconciled to us after subtracting some of his righteousness; on the contrary by the very fulfilment and revelation of his righteousness he has placed us in a new position, we have been reconciled, taken out of an impossible relationship to him and placed in the only possible relationship. This condition of our salvation (or positively: our life) has been fulfilled through God's verdict, and that is the truly wonderful fact that continues to engage Paul in Chapter 5.

For two reasons this is a difficult chapter, so far as its subject-matter is concerned – perhaps the most difficult in the whole Epistle to the Romans. First, because unfortunately it is not natural for us to see how unheard-of, how incomprehensible, how simply miraculous it is that there is such a thing as people who are reconciled with God, and that we are such people. It is not natural for us to see this in its reality and at the same time in the whole wonder of its reality, because we are much more accustomed to accepting it with doubts or else with a most inappropriate levity, as if it were a matter of course. And secondly it is a difficult chapter because unfortunately we are just as vague about the fact that this has nothing to do with a general idea of God and of man, but that on the contrary it is a particular fact, the fact of the person of Jesus Christ, and as such so miraculous and at the same time so real. Paul stands before that fact *amazed*, without any reserve, he stands before it as this definite *fact*, he stands before Jesus Christ. Nowhere else in the Epistle is this expressed so emphatically as it is in this chapter. It is this that makes the chapter so difficult for us to follow. In our Christian thinking (even though it be very 'positive') we are no longer accustomed to this certainty and this wonder and, particularly, this concentration on the person of Jesus Christ. The distance between our way of thinking and the apostles' can become very evident here – not because the one is ancient and the other modern but because we have to rediscover not only the object but also the categories of the apostles' way of thinking. Perhaps the first and most important thing we have to learn from this chapter is that we have much to learn if we are to be intelligent pupils of the Apostles.

The contents of 5.1-5 seem comparatively simple and clear. First in 5.1 we have before us the connection with what has preceded it: as men who have been justified in faith we have *peace* with God so that an end has been made of all that, according to the plain words in 5.10, formed our enmity towards God – our rebellion against him in which (1.21) we deny him the honour due to him and so – whatever that may mean to him – at any rate plunge ourselves into misery, give ourselves into the power of death (5.12ff). When God has justified us, we are acquitted of that enmity and placed in a state of peace, of agreement with him. In what sense? Paul is not referring to peaceful sentiments or emotions which may dominate us but to Jesus Christ as the One in whom has been completed not only (5.2) our access to God and our justification but also this making our peace with God, however things may look within us. Never mind about sentiments and emotions: the point at issue is the 'peace of God which passeth all understanding' (Phil. 4.7) so that we can be confident that we have made peace, we have peace with God. We are *not* those enemies of God. Certainly not in Jesus Christ: he is at peace with God and he himself 'is *our* peace' (Eph. 2.14). Because he has placed us in that state of grace in which we are allowed to be, he *is* our peace. That is why it is all so certain, that is why it cannot be called into question either by ourselves or by anyone else or by any power in heaven and on earth (8.36ff). Because we have that peace, we look into our future and discover that what we have before us is God's glory. Therefore we praise our present life because it is hastening towards that future. We do not only praise the future which is ours, not only the eternity of the life to come (5.3) but also the afflicted present, because all affliction can only make the man who has peace with God more steadfast, more persistent. In such steadfastness he will prove true and this steadfastness will be worth while because he now hopes even more truly and sincerely. Only now does he hope really seriously: in that hope which will not be put to shame, which will not confound the one who hopes. For what holds him in fact? A new feeling, willing and knowing? No, no matter whether he has much of it or not. What holds him is the objective power of the love which God has shown him by (5.5) placing him, in Jesus Christ, apart from and against all his feeling, willing and knowing, in a position where he is allowed to find himself in harmony with God. By the Holy Spirit, which has awakened and called man to faith, the favour of God's love has been poured out into his heart. It is now wholly full of this favour, however weak and evil it may yet be, so that right across all the grumbling, sighing and complaining that may be natural to it – it can only pour out praise – the praise of the hope, the praise of the future glory of God, who is for us, of whom we are sure, and also the praise of all the affliction of the present, because it can only increase and never diminish the hope of the man who has peace with God.

This astonishment of the Apostle which is so extraordinary to us, is particularly emphasized in 5.6-11, and in connection with it the absolute certainty with which he approaches the fact that men can have peace with God and may consequently live in hope. The more amazing this is the more certain it is – because it passes all understanding it is also a sure peace; that is a summary of what is stated here. And what about the love of God which fills our hearts, in the strength of which we have been reconciled and have that peace? Paul replies in 5.8 by stating: God proves it by the fact that Christ died for us when we were yet sinners, 'while we were yet weak, at the time when we were yet ungodly' (5.6), as Abraham (4.4)! 'While we were his enemies we were reconciled to God through the death of his Son' (5.10)! Such is the love which fills and governs our hearts through the Holy Spirit: not the understandable and intelligible love which a man has for his best friend for whom he might – or might not – be prepared to die (5.7) and consequently not a love of which we might have some knowledge and experience otherwise. In other words, not our human love by which we love those who love us in return, but God's love, which is love of his enemies. We can now understand why the peace of God ought not to be confused with peaceful sentiments and emotions. That makes this love and the peace which it creates in us incomprehensible, wonderful. The act of God, in which he gives up his Son for us in order to adopt us in his Son's place, the act which brings us peace, is an act of such love: God is for us, while we are against God. In Jesus Christ this is true, and through the Holy Spirit it has been poured out into our hearts so that our hearts are full of it, so full that they must break forth into the mere praise of our eternal glory, into the mere praise even of the afflicted present. That is what amazes Paul.

But this amazement does not make him doubt! We might doubt our Christian sentiments and emotions, and the conclusions we could draw from them. We might doubt everything that our human love produces in uplift and comfort. But that which God is and does: the verdict which as such is the manifestation of his love – the manifestation of his love which as such is his just verdict – that is so great, that is so much its own proof in its greatness, that it is not merely indubitable, but simply compels us to the certain knowledge that 'In his blood we are saved by him from the threatening wrath of God' (5.9). Our *future* is that we have been saved by him in his blood! And the prospect of the *present* is accordingly: God in his love of his enemies, the blood of his Son shed for us sinners, that is our future, our hope. This God is coming, God in the form of this Man, the One who in his death has already suffered, borne and taken away all righteous wrath. In him everything that speaks against us has been refuted. In him all our evil enmity towards God has already been done away with! He has already gone through and got through all the misery, the darkness of death which is the result of that enmity! And moreover: he has done this entirely without us and in spite of us, so that we cannot and need not now ask how it is possible from our side to have peace with God, that we can be reconciled with God in spite of everything we are and do! In him it became true that in spite of ourselves we are reconciled!

This proof of what we are to look forward to and therefore the meaning of the present has compelling force because it is so absolutely amazing. Paul argues twice (5.9, 10) 'that if the greater thing from God's side is real and true, how much more must the smaller thing too be real and true to us'. The greater thing is the miracle of God's love of his enemies, unmerited, unfounded and inexplicable by any human reasons, wholly different from any love and any miracles we may come across otherwise. The smaller thing is our peace, our reconciliation, out future salvation and therefore the glory and the praise of our hearts which have been filled with the love of God. It is well-founded, divinely founded and therefore absolutely well-founded in the greater thing that God has done from his side – it is well-founded in God's being God.

In 5.12-21[1] it is emphasized that it is the one Man Jesus Christ in whom God's decision about man (as described in 5.1-11) has been made and revealed: Jesus Christ is the One who has reversed and annulled that other decision made by man himself: man's entering into his enmity to God and into the misery of death which is the result of that enmity, Jesus Christ made good the evil that Adam had committed. We can understand the passage if we go immediately from 5.12 to 5.18 and then to 5.21. For the first sentence in 5.12 is either incomplete, or, more probably, forms a kind of heading: 'As in the case of the one man through whom sin came into the world, and through sin death and therefore the extension of death to all men – so in the case of the one man Jesus Christ!' The meaning is that the whole history of mankind as determined by Adam and his fall, that whole repetition of his sin and his misery in those who collectively and individually bear his name, the name 'man', is one single parable of what has happened in Jesus Christ, in virtue of the righteousness and love of God. A parable, an example (5.14) – just that and no more – to be considered by us as such and no more! This also applies to our own share in it, also to all enmity towards God and all the corresponding misery which we think we discover in ourselves certainly not without reason. It applies to our whole existence, if we want to overlook the fact that we believe and in that faith may receive our acquittal and live by and in that acquittal. For the whole argument is only meant to be and only allowed to be a reminder of Jesus Christ. It is a reminder of God's decision which is victorious over Adam's decision, by which the latter is reversed, annulled and undone. 5.18-19 and 21 contain the heart of what Paul wants to say here in accordance with the heading in 5.12. Through the transgression of one man came the condemnation of all men, and in the same way, through the righteous deed of one Man, came the acquittal of all. The

[1] For this text cf. *Christus und Adam* (Theologische Studien, Vol. 35, 1952), ET, *Christ and Adam* (*S.J.T.* Occasional Papers No. 5, Edinburgh, 1956).

disobedience of one man placed the many in the position of sinners before God, and the obedience again of one Man placed the many in the position of righteous men.

In both cases there are the one and the many. Here is the one who with what he is, does and suffers is the witness to that which the many, are, do and have to suffer – here there are all, the many, who must recognize themselves only too well in that which the one man was, did and suffered. And in the other case, too, there is the One who represents all, the many – and again there are all, the many who are allowed to recognize themselves in this one Man. In the one case the existence of the one produced for all, for the many, the dominion of sin and death – in the other the existence of the One produces for all, for the many, the dominion of grace through righteousness unto eternal life (5.21). Note that Paul does not simply place Adam and Christ – all in the first case and all in the other – in juxtaposition as if they were figures and factors of equal dignity and equal value and as if they were the bearers of an equally powerful destiny. Adam and his many are meant to stand by the side of Christ and his many merely as a parable. He precedes Christ merely as a shadow and an example. He is only apparently the first. The first is Jesus Christ. He is in possession of the reality which the other can only copy, and must copy in all his complete difference in kind. There is here no question of power against power, of right against right, let alone of God against God. This is God against man because he is for man. This is right against injustice, truth against the lie, power against impotence – but in such a manner that injustice must witness to the right, the lie to the truth, the impotence to power, sinful man to the gracious God; in such a manner that God and what he does for man is reflected, yea revealed in what man has desired to do and has done against God.

Here God's righteousness and love are victorious by becoming visible and glorious in the figure and parable of human iniquity and enmity. That this is what Paul means is made clear in 5.15-17 where he keeps pointing out how entirely different the two partners and their work for all, for the many, really are, how the grace of God and the sin and punishment of man (5.15), God's grace and God's judgment (5.16), the dominion of life and the dominion of death (5.17), do *not* in fact counter-balance each other, do not equally possess the character of reality. Paul points out how the latter is in fact counteracted and annulled, overcome, surpassed, defeated and done away with. These partners and their work for all, for the many, must therefore be seen and understood in this dissimilarity. The same intention is shown even more clearly in 5.13-14 and 20. These verses declare that even the revelation and enactment of the Law – apparently a terrible aggravation of the conflict, the immortalization of Adam's sin and of the judgment pronounced on him – could in reality (as we were shown in a different manner in 1.18–3.20) only serve and in fact did serve the revelation of God's gracious decision. For grace became exceedingly abundant at the very place where the transgression of man, through its encounter with the holy will of God, became visible and manifest in its form as enmity towards God, which deserves death.

This and only this is the significance of all that speaks against us because of the whole human reality of ours which is called 'Adam' and therefore 'dominion of sin and subjection to death'. The image of him who speaks for us is able to show us that reality! The divine Victor is reflected in our human defeat! Human sin witnesses to God's grace too, particularly when it is shown up, as it must be most clearly, in the light of God's will and Law. And death, which is its inevitable result, pre-eminently witnesses to eternal life: that is to say, when all this reality of Adam is confronted by Jesus Christ, when it is measured by him and considered with him in view. The presupposition of the whole argument is that it *is* in fact confronted by him, and that therefore it cannot call in question our reconciliation with God, the peace of God which we *have*, but can only *confirm* it. If the decision that has been made in Jesus Christ, if faith in him is final, then no other supposition is possible and consequently no other result for Adam and his whole world.

The Gospel as Man's Sanctification

THE sixth chapter gives a second explanation of the statement in 1.16 that the Gospel of God is God's almighty *work of salvation* for everyone who believes. One can also say that it is a second explanation of 1.17, that the man who is righteous before God through his faith shall live in that faith. For the *salvation* of man by God's grace, by the divine verdict, made and pronounced in the Gospel, consists in the fact that man may *live* and may indeed live eternally, indefinitely, beyond all fear and power of death (5.21; 6.23). Chapter 5 has elucidated this by describing the man who is righteous before God by means of his faith, as the man who is *reconciled* with God: he is God's enemy who, thanks to God's inexplicable love, has been made his friend (5.1-11), so radically and truly that he can now only look back on that whole realm of enmity towards God, on the whole world of the first Adam as an example and parable of the infinitely more true and real dominion of grace and life under which he is now allowed to be according to the divine verdict (5.12-21).

We may explain Chapter 6 as follows. The man who is righteous before God through his faith is the man who has been sanctified by God (6.19, 23). We can provisionally define this idea in the following way. As a man who has been reconciled with God he has really been put into another, into a new, position, not by his own effort but by the decision of God who placed him there – but even so he himself.

The light from Jesus Christ which has touched him from

without has not merely touched him on the outside, it has penetrated him. Man has been told that he is righteous, not merely as far as appearances go, but seriously, with the whole power of God's creative word. 'The love of God has been poured out into our *hearts*' (5.5), not in the form of particular sentiments and emotions, but in the form of a truly different existence, another, new constitution. To this man himself – in the Bible the 'heart' is man himself – has been made subject, and therefore all his inner and outer life too. He who is righteous by means of his faith 'walks in a new life' (6.4), not *by* his own decision (how could he have arrived at that?), but, all the same, *by means of* his own decision which has become inevitable because God has decided that he is no longer God's enemy but God's friend. Man's own decision has become a matter of course, because he himself, his heart, has received a new destiny: the destiny which is determined by God's love which fills the heart. That destiny is man's *sanctification*. Sanctification is entirely God's grace. It is not man's affair, but God's – the affair of the God who works for man in Jesus Christ. No man can take it for himself. No man can desire it of his own accord, no one can shape or accomplish it in any way. The sixth chapter makes this unmistakably clear. It says that God's grace, the work of the God who acts in Jesus Christ on our behalf, in fact consists in our actually living a new life, in our already being other men. It says that this new *being* is also the *order* under which we live and in sole obedience to which we can live: it is the claim and the command which entirely monopolize us and which we therefore have to obey. Rom. 6 does not say that we have to realize our sanctification by our obedience. How can we make it real? In the same way as our reconciliation it has been realized as our sanctification in Jesus Christ, once and for all, and therefore there is no need for reiteration or confirmation (6.10). It is true that 'he has been made unto us sanctification' (I Cor. 1.30) and that he has been made the order which we have to respect as the already established truth about our existence. This is the theme developed in Rom. 6 from the same central point of view and in the same sense as we learned in Rom. 5 that we have peace with God.

The chapter is clearly divided in two parts: 6.1-14 and 15-23. The theme is the same in both: the man who has been sanctified by the Gospel. But the emphasis is different. In 6.1-14 (where we find the quintessence, the substance proper of the chapter), emphasis is put upon the fact that the new position of the man who is righteous before God through his faith consists in a new *being*. And in 6.15-23 it is emphasized that the new position is a new *order* to be respected obediently. But it is all-important to realize that this is merely a change of emphasis and that there is no question of one thing having to be followed by another, of a completion of God's goodwill by our human willingness, or of the division: 'This I did for you; what do you do for me?' For the new being, as is already perfectly clear in 6.1-14, is in itself and as such the new *order* of human life which is to be respected obediently. And in 6.15-23 the only motive for respecting the new order is that the new order is our new *being*, the law of which we cannot escape however much we try, any more than we can stand in the air instead of on the firm ground. Here as well as there (6.14, 23) the subject is God's *grace*: the fact that God's grace is our sanctification and that as such it leaves nothing to be desired and cannot be surpassed in sincerity and thoroughness, in the way it comforts and disturbs man. Here as well as there the point is the confirmation and development of the statement in 3.31: that we establish the *Law* through *faith*.

The division of the chapter into these two parts is indicated by the question in 6.1 and 15 being mentioned twice. In both cases it is substantially the same question: we are subject to God's grace. Are we to, *ought* we perhaps even to continue in sin, to desire sin, so that this grace may become more powerfully, more gloriously triumphant over sin? We have met that question before, in 3.7-8, and we remember how, since it was a fool's question, it was not answered but duly crushed. Though at first sight it may appear likely, it does not really seem that we must regard Rom. 6 as a belated reply to that question. Here too the reply which it receives is (6.1 and 15) simply the one word 'impossible', 'God forbid'. Any discussion even is impossible. For how can one discuss[1] when one is already separated? The explanation which follows the 'impossible' in 6.2ff and 16ff was in truth not inspired by its contradiction of the question or of the positive statement hidden in the question. It is necessary and needed for its own sake as a positive explanation of an important aspect of the Gospel.

The foolish assertion which is concealed in the question can only emerge once more as something that is 'impossible'. It signalizes, as it were, the existence of the unsanctified man, who would hear the Gospel with unsanctified ears and receive and repeat it with unsanctified lips, although the Gospel is the sanctification of man, although the Gospel in particular should in no circumstances be heard and repeated in this manner, and such questions ought therefore not to be asked in any circumstances. For the question is about a sin in which man would want to persist and with a grace which man would be able to increase by his actions, i.e. by his persisting in sin. But that is neither the sin that has been condemned and abrogated by the Gospel, nor the grace which the Gospel grants. To ask that kind of question is consciously or unconsciously to revile the Gospel. And the question can only be interesting and worth mentioning because for all its foolishness it does show that the genuine Gospel has been preached and has encountered the unsanctified man. Whenever that happens, this question emerges and the unholiness of the man who hears the Gospel is shown by his effort to keep the Gospel at arm's length with this question. The emergence of this question could almost be regarded as a criterion for the authenticity of the preaching of the Gospel. Wherever the true Gospel is preached, the fools are sure to ask this question. Wherever they do not ask this question, there is at least room for a serious suspicion that something very differ-

---

[1] In German '*sich auseinandersetzen*', literally 'separate themselves one from the other'. *Translator*.

ent from the Gospel has perhaps been preached. A gospel that is not reviled by this question can hardly be the genuine Gospel. And therefore the question is put here twice, more or less as a signal: the authentic Gospel is at issue. And at the same time as a warning: the Gospel does not really look like its reflected image in the distorting mirror of this question. On the contrary, the Gospel is concerned with the sanctification of that very unsanctified man who can ask the question, who cannot help asking it.

After mentioning this question (6.1) the first part (6.1-14) starts with an abrupt statement, produced in the form of a counter-question: we, who have died to sin, shall live in sin no longer. This means that we have a death behind us, our own death inasmuch as our life has been our life in, under and for sin. And we have a life before us which will in any case no longer be that life depleted by death. Man lives in this present, with that past behind him and this future before him, and this is his sanctification.

But what kind of present is that? Paul replies that it is the present life of the man who has been baptized in the name of Jesus Christ. His past, his origin is simply that (as his baptism testifies) he has been received into fellowship with Jesus Christ. And therefore all that which happened in Jesus Christ once and for all for all mankind now also applies to him, now also profits him. But that which happened in Jesus Christ, happened in his death. And the man baptized in the name of Jesus Christ has therefore been baptized in his death. That is, by the death of Jesus Christ something has happened, which has also happened for him, which is also applicable to him, which also profits him. His baptism therefore attested his own burial (6.4), which has taken place in and with that of the slain body of Christ in the tomb of Joseph of Arimathaea. What, therefore, can be the future of the man who has been baptized? Evidently only something corresponding and comparable with, something resembling the resurrection of Jesus Christ from the dead,

68

founded on the resurrection of Christ in the same way as his death and burial were founded on Christ's death and burial: a change to a new life which is no continuation of the old but surpasses it in every respect. In our baptism (6.5) we have 'grown together' ('become united', AV) with the likeness of his death, as we have become part of one large reflected image of his death and burial to such an extent that we can quite seriously be said to have died at Golgotha, and to have been buried in that garden. Surely the same must be true about his resurrection. The reflected image of his resurrection of which we are part, with which thanks to our baptism we have 'grown together' is the new life in which since our baptism we do not merely have to move but in which in fact we do move, we do walk towards the future.

What does all that mean? Well, we know (6.6) – this is our knowledge of Jesus Christ on which our faith is founded – that the 'old man', i.e. we ourselves, as God's enemies, have been crucified and killed in and with the crucifixion of the man Jesus at Golgotha, so that the 'body' (i.e. the subject, the person needed for the doing) of sin, the man who can sin and will and shall sin has been removed, destroyed, done away with, is simply no longer there (and has therefore not merely been 'made powerless'). We can no longer be servants of sin because the man who could do that – and who could do nothing except be a servant of sin – is simply no longer alive, is simply no longer there. Further service of sin would be a self-contradictory and impossible effort to undo our past and to revive the old man who by virtue of our baptism is already dead and buried. Sin no longer has any right, any claim on the man who has this death behind him – the death of Jesus Christ, which by virtue of his baptism has also happened for him (6.7). He has been released from its service, and even should he want to resume it – this is a legal question which has been decided – he would not be able to do so. What he has before him can in any case (6.8) only be a life with Christ, a life corresponding with Christ's resurrection, freed from the service of sin: as surely as

Christ who was raised from the dead (6.9) has no further death before him, as surely as death has no more claim on him and no more power over him, as surely (6.10) as Christ, who was laden with our sin, who atoned for our sin, who suffered the punishment for our sin, has died once and for all to sin, as surely as he now lives to face God, God alone and certainly not a future death – the everlasting, the eternal life of the man who was raised to the right hand of the Father. What else is left to the man who was baptized in Christ, but the present from which he has to view his past and his future as described in the amazing statement of 6.2? What other view or opinion of himself (6.11) is allowed and possible for him but that as far as sin is concerned I am dead, gone, simply not there any more, I have been cut off and separated from sin. Because I no longer live for sin, I now live for God who has cut me off from sin. This happened in Jesus Christ because in truth I belong to that reflected image of his death and life – because in truth what happened to him happened *for me*, with such authority and legitimacy that, whatever may be done on my part or by me, has not only been covered but annulled by that which was done for me. I am no longer my own responsibility but his. I am no longer my own property but his. That is the view and judgment of ourselves which belongs to the faith (6.8), in which we recognize our sanctification. From it we shall never be able to derive anything concerning all that is happening through us and to us except (6.12) that sin may no longer reign 'in our mortal body', i.e. in what is as yet our mortal form here and now, as subjects which are distinguished from the Subject Jesus Christ. It may not do this because it cannot, because in this very form we have been baptized. We have 'grown together' with the reflected image of his death and his resurrection and have therefore died to sin. We have been cut off from sin, we have been snatched away from the dominion of sin. The desires which are peculiar to this our mortal form as such have no legitimate claim on our obedience because in this our mortal form we already no longer belong to ourselves but to Jesus

Christ. Even here and now the subject which otherwise should be and would be subject and obedient to sin is no longer alive, because even in this dying form we have no other future before us than the one we have by belonging to Jesus Christ.

From this view and judgment of ourselves follows the prohibition: 'Do not make available your members (the possibilities and expressions of your lives in every respect) as instruments of iniquity.'

Further follows the commandment: 'But present yourselves to God (as that which you are) as men who have come to life from the dead and make available your members as instruments of righteousness unto God' (6.13). Do not do the former, you cannot do it. Do the latter because it is the only possibility, because sin (6.14) shall not reign over you. Note the explanation of the imperative by the indicative. Never in any circumstances shall sin have a legitimate claim, a genuine dominion over you, even if you do the former and not the latter. With you, the baptized, there can never be any motive for sin. With you least of all! You are not under the Law, which might accuse you of sin, which might confirm that you are sinners. You are under grace, by which you have been acquitted of sin, because even the Judge himself has not spoken against you but for you and has therefore pronounced God's verdict as regards you and executed it already. Your sanctification is such that it has happened independently of your good or bad will, because the 'no' to sin and the 'yes' to a new life that has no more interest in sin, that has turned to God, is fixed for ever and is therefore valid already here and now. You must, you shall therefore no longer live the old life but move in the new life. For you have no other! You only have the life in fellowship with him who has taken sin, your sin, unto himself and who has done away with it, and who now has only the life with God before him. This is the power of the imperative of your sanctification.

After mentioning the fool's question (6.15) once more, the second section (6.15-23) emphasizes that those who are, according to 6.14, in a state of grace and therefore subject to a definite order, have been brought into a relationship of service. Note that Paul says in 6.19 that this is a 'human way' of regarding it, adopted 'because of the weakness of your flesh', which he has introduced to make himself understood completely and surely, and at all events practically, just in case that which was said in 6.1-14 had not become sufficiently comprehensible. At the same time he warned his readers that the comprehensible, practical words which follow were not to be understood in an abstract sense, that they should only be heard and understood in the light of, as an application of, what was said there.

We are told in 6.16 that man has a lord, one way or the other. He is either a servant of sin, or a servant of obedience. Sin and obedience are therefore not in the first place our actions, but powers which have dominion over us. But the grace of God, which can never be praised enough, is (6.17) that though we were servants of sin, we are so no longer; for when we were told and when we heard the Gospel, we have become obedient to it with all our heart and therefore with our whole existence. We have therefore become subjects of that second realm, servants of obedience: freed from sin and made servants of righteousness. Servants? Here Paul inserts (6.19) the remark that in this new state we are, properly speaking, not dealing with slavery but with freedom. In any case the fact that we are no longer servants of sin can be made clear by the fact that we do now live under another dominion, in another realm, that now we are 'servants of liberty'. That is more or less the substance of what Paul here wants to say figuratively, 'in a human way'. Once again the old life of bondage to sin that is gone (5.12f) is made a symbol of the life that we have before us, now as then! Now: this better parallel to the dominion under which we were then is our sanctification, the life under God's 'yes' by which our life under God's 'no' has been overtaken, surpassed and destroyed. And then in 6.20-22 there is the contrast: as you had a lord then and have a Lord now, so you were then also free, i.e. from righteousness – a terrible freedom, the inevitable shameful result and fruit of which is death. And in the same way you are free again, i.e. from sin, because you have become servants of God, with the result that by his decision and by the ensuing order, you are sanctified men who, as such, are on the way to eternal life. Therefore death is the reward, the wages in one case (6.23), life everlasting is the gift of grace in the other. You are no hirelings, no paid workers, you receive and have the gift of grace. This receiving and having is your life and as such is the order under which you live, the imperative which you have to obey, because apart from this order you do not even exist. Because this is true, the Gospel is from this point of view too inevitably and as such your sanctification.

The Gospel as Man's Liberation

CHAPTER 7[1] produces a further, third explanation of the statement in 1.16 that the Gospel is God's almighty *work of salvation*, to everyone who believes. It is a third explanation of the thesis in 1.17 that the man who by his faith is righteous before God shall *live*. We now learn that the Gospel is man's liberation, i.e. his liberation from the *law*. This we read in the decisive verse of the parable at the beginning of the chapter (7.3), and then also in retrospect at the beginning of the next (8.2). But the text in 8.2 in particular immediately warns us to be exact. It says there that we have been liberated from the '*law of sin and death*' and if we want to understand Rom. 7, it should not be overlooked anywhere, that it is this law that is at issue and no other. We have been liberated from this law, we are released and exempt, yea dead to that law. That is what the chapter actually says, and what we find contained in the first part (7.1-6) and confirmed in the last (7.24-25). The rest is not a continuation of that main statement, but an elucidation in two paragraphs (7.7-12 and 13-23) of the particular sense in which the law is meant in 7.1-6, and therefore of the particular sense in which we who believe in the Gospel are said to have been liberated from the law. Compare 8.2 with 7.7 and 7.13, and it is obvious that the second and third parts of Chapter 7 elucidate how and in how far the Law can be (1) a law of *sin*, and (2) a law of *death*, from which the Gospel has liberated us.

Chapter 7 has always been one of the most noted and empha-

[1] Cf. *KD*, IV, 1, p. 648f. (E.T. p. 581f.)

sized parts of the Epistle to the Romans. There would be nothing against that, on the contrary much could be said for it if our own attention had been directed to the extraordinary import of the knowledge of our liberation from the law of sin and death as expressed in 7.1-6 and 24-25. It does not show a very good understanding of the Epistle that the particular interest of so many readers has not been focused on that main statement but on its added elucidations and especially on 7.13-23, where the law from which we have been liberated is described more particularly as the law of death, i.e. as the law which condemns us to death. A most interesting, most exciting psychology of sin was supposed to be found there. It was overlooked in the process that 7.13-23 as well as 7.7-12 are, so to speak, additional notes in smaller print in which Paul describes the meaning and the action of that law from which by our faith we have in fact been liberated – or rather for which in our faith we ourselves are no longer available. These verses therefore picture a situation which can only interest us as our past situation which is outdated in the faith, a situation in which we did not have the right attitude to sin or to the Law. And Paul's words about it certainly do not invite us to remain in that situation or to take it seriously. He does not desire to draw our attention to what *prevails and happens* in the situation from which we have been called away in the faith, but to the fact that we have been *called away* from it. In other words, he draws our attention to the fact that we cannot, believing in the Gospel, hope to find anything in the field of psychology – certainly no grace and life, not even the knowledge of our real sin. What, actually, is the real importance of this realm? That in the faith in the Gospel it is behind us. That this realm *is behind us*, is the theme of Rom. 7, in the sections 7-12 and 13-23 as well.

The main statement of 7.1-6 begins in 7.1 with a retrospective question: 'or do you not know, brethren . . .' – the decisive sequel is according to 7.6: 'that we have been discharged and released, that we are exempt from the law?' As Paul evidently thinks that his readers do not know this well or clearly enough,

75

he adds this further explanation: the Gospel is God's almighty work of salvation also in the sense that it is man's liberation, his liberation from the law. The question evidently refers back to a certain passage in Chapter 6, i.e. 6.14 (cf. 6.15), where Paul had argued the proposition that 'sin will not have dominion over you' from the other proposition that 'you are not under the law, but under grace'. In Chapter 6 Paul says that we are not allowed to sin any longer, because we cannot do so any more. We cannot do it any more, because as men who were able to sin we have died in the death of Jesus Christ and are no longer available, because by the resurrection of Jesus Christ we have been placed under an order which excludes sin. This proposition had first emerged in this context, only to disappear again.

It had anticipated what will now be discussed more in detail: you may not, you cannot sin any longer, because when you yourself, the old man, died with Jesus Christ in his death, the actual 'power' of sin (as Paul says in I Cor. 15.56), i.e. the law, lost its dominion over you, because you who have died and risen with Jesus Christ are under grace and no longer under the law. Paul had hinted at that before: 'Where there is no law there is no transgression' (4.15). But he seems to suspect that this knowledge when put forward in merely parenthetic and allusive statements of this kind might easily be lacking in the illuminating power it ought to have. He evidently suspects that other things which he has said equally parenthetically about the law may have made far more impression on his readers or may even seem most cryptically to contradict these statements, i.e. 'the law works wrath' (4.15), or: 'the law came in between so that the trespass has become exceedingly great' (5.20). He evidently suspects that all that has been said in Chapter 6 of the Gospel as man's sanctification might be over-shadowed and threatened by the question whether, in spite of the death and resurrection of Jesus Christ, in spite of our faith in him and our baptism in his name the law does not – now as before – continue to bring sin to life and keep it alive, whether it does not continue to accuse us of being sinners and belie our sanctification and therefore our reconciliation with God, and consequently the whole work of salvation of the Gospel and God's verdict that in the faith in Jesus Christ we are righteous in his sight. Is the law still there in this capacity, as this danger to believers? This it is which Paul denies in Chapter 7. It is denied by the statement that we have been liberated from the law, i.e. from the law of sin and death. But this statement needs some elucidation. The sections 7.7-12 and 13-23 serve to elucidate the assumption we had here, that the law incites us to sin and on the other hand accuses us of sin and condemns us to death. But before it can be elucidated the statement must first be made explicitly. That is done in 7.1-6 and in the concluding verses, 7.24-25.

7.1 begins with the assertion, known and obvious to anyone who knows what a law is: that the law has in mind and governs the living man. That a man's death, therefore, annuls all his obligations to others as well as all the obligations of others to him. The living man to whom Paul is referring, who is therefore subject to the law, is man 'in the flesh' (7.5), who therefore lives as 'the old man' (6.6). The law no doubt applies to him and binds him: the 'law of sin and death' (8.2), the only law with which, according to the question he has to answer, Paul is concerned. It is the law, which on the one hand (according to 7.5) provokes the desires of sin in our members, in our whole life, and on the other (6.21) causes the fear of death by the verdict it pronounces on us. The *life* of this man will always and in any circumstances be his life under this law. In 7.2 a parable commences. As long as this man – the husband, it now says – is alive, his wife is tied to him by the law which binds him – and which, as long as he is alive, binds her as well. In other words, as long as we (the husband) live in the flesh as that old man, we (the wife) are governed by the law, that binds him and therefore ourselves, we are in fact bound to become sinners properly speaking because of the law and to be accused as such by the law. As long as he is alive, the law of the living husband is our law as well. But when he (i.e. we ourselves inasmuch as we live in the flesh) dies, then the wife is free, not only from him, but also from that law which bound both him and her. That is inasmuch as by the death of the old man we have been placed in a new situation, we are then no longer bound by that necessity: then the law has lost for us its power as instigator and accuser of our sin. Of course (7.3) the husband's death is necessary for the wife to become free legitimately. Were she to seize that liberty and belong to another man while her husband was still alive, then the law which binds them both would accuse and condemn her as an adulteress. In other words, without the death of the old man any attempt to withdraw from the law of sin and death, any attempt to escape sin and death could only result in our being, more than ever, convicted of sin and condemned to death by that same law. As long as we live in the flesh, what do we achieve in this direction but that which the OT calls Israel's qualified adultery against its God: every kind of idolatry and every kind of confidence in our own works, sin, which does not expel sin but brings it to perfection and which can only make our sentence of death irrevocable? But by his death the wife can in fact become free of the law which ties her to her husband. And according to the same law that tied her to her first husband, she can then belong to someone else, without being charged with adultery. In other words, we can actually and therefore legitimately and properly be free of the law of sin and death by no longer existing, by no longer being available as those who lived in the flesh, because we are killed and dead, so that the law which applied to the old man no longer applies to us. This means that we now can be different men, no longer under the dominion of that law, no longer affected by the law's inducing and condemning of sin, but liberated men.

7.3-6 contain the interpretation of the parable. It starts with its final part. The thing that sets the wife free from her husband and therefore from her own obligation to the law, has happened to the believers. According to 6.2ff they have been released from the law of sin and death, because their old man was killed, killed together with and in the bodily killing of Jesus Christ. But here the parable proves inadequate. For with that death of theirs in Jesus Christ they have not, as the wife, merely received the liberty to belong to *just anybody* else. The purpose of that death was that they should belong to *someone quite definite*: to the One with whom they have died, who is also the One who was raised from the dead; so that in this legitimate and necessary new bond and relationship they might bear fruit unto God and no longer unto death. The effect of the law, that it provokes sin and condemns it, from which they cannot escape, from which they only desire to escape but which all their attempts to escape can only make worse, has become past history to them, because they themselves (inasmuch as their life in the flesh is concerned) have become past history. It has become the past, as only death can create the past (7.6) – not just any death (for death as such could only create a vacuum) but the death of Jesus Christ. He does not only untie that which binds, the bonds, the existence to which the law has tied men, but as truly as he has risen from the dead, he at the same time sets free the man who has died that death for this entirely different bond – for the service in this new condition of the Spirit, which begins exactly where the old condition of the letter, i.e. the application and effect of the law, ends. 'Thanks be to God through our Lord Jesus Christ,' Paul was to exclaim at the end of the chapter (7.25) – 'thanks be to God who snatched me, wretched man that I am, from the "body of this death",' i.e. from this human existence which the law had inescapably destined to death, from which I could not and cannot save myself, about which I could only sigh. Even now, while looking back upon it as my past, I can only sigh, 'Who shall deliver me from it?' But in Jesus Christ I have been delivered from that existence by means of the death which he has prepared for this body of death, which my existence has undergone in him (7.24). As the dead past, as my own past, it may still be my existence. It may still be there for God's eyes and my own. It may be that in the flesh – in my flesh that has been abandoned to death in Jesus Christ – I daily serve that 'law of sin' until my end. But in my inner self in which I find I am alive in the life of Jesus Christ, I myself am already now serving the Law of God (7.25), I am really free from the law which is the law of sin and death, however much it may be the law to which even now I see my flesh subjected, that was killed in Jesus Christ. What the life is like in this other service, in the new condition of the Spirit, Paul discusses in Chapter 8, and he then explains from a fourth aspect how the Gospel is God's almighty work of salvation.

In the remaining larger part of Chapter 7 Paul gives two elucidations of the main statement he has made in 7.1-6 concerning the law, that the law from which we have been liberated is the 'law of sin and death'. Only on this assumption can there be any question of a liberation from the law. It is only from this law that the believer can be free. We know that Paul has no intention of annulling the Law, but of establishing it through the faith (3.31), through the proclamation of the Gospel. In the preceding chapter he certainly established the Law firmly enough! And in this chapter too he says that as far as the Law is concerned there is in this newly-gained freedom no question of lawlessness, but of service in a new condition (7.6). And at the end of the chapter he says emphatically that in his inner being he himself (as distinguished from his dead life in the flesh) is allowed to serve the Law of God and does in fact serve it (7.25). And later (8.2) he was to express himself even more strongly: that it is this very Law of God ('the Law of Spirit and life') that liberates man from the law of sin and death. But what about the law of sin and death? How can we explain the existence of that law of which we can only say in the end that the Gospel liberates us from it, that as believers we are *not* subject to it. What are its functions?

'Is the Law sin?' Paul is asked (7.7), and with a shudder (the same shudder as in 6.2, 15) he answers: 'Impossible!' (EVV: 'God forbid!'). The Law is (3.21) the confirmation of the

Gospel, the form, the shell in which the Gospel comes to us men. How could the Gospel come to us but in the form of exhortation, warning, instruction, decree, commandment and prohibition? Paul himself has applied it in this form – the form of the Law – for the proclamation of the judgment of all men, pronounced in the Gospel. In all his epistles and consequently in the Epistle to the Romans too, Paul himself preached the Law as this form of the Gospel. As a form of the Gospel, far from being sin, the Law is the form in which God's grace is revealed. And as such it is holy, and what it commands – each one of its commandments – is holy and just and good (7.12). But the Law (and the Gospel in the form of the Law) is proclaimed in the realm of sin. It is given to sinful man. Because of the dominion of sin in his eyes, ears and hands, it becomes that other law from which he has to be liberated and from which he is in fact liberated by that which as God's Law it includes the Gospel, by the faith which in the Law receives and accepts the Gospel. It belongs to God's condescension that in the Law as the form of the Gospel he exposes himself to sin, to human misunderstanding and abuse. It belongs to his holiness that the form of his grace abused by sinful man becomes the instrument of his wrath and judgment of man, that the man who is guilty of that abuse, is even in this abused form confronted with God himself, only that he must now experience that God is not to be mocked. And it belongs to God's mercy and his omnipotence that in the end he does not acquiesce in the abuse of that form of his grace, that he does not leave it to be abused by man, but that in Jesus Christ he makes the Gospel, hidden in the Law, come out of its profaned shell. Thus he causes the Law to arise again and to be disclosed anew as *his* Law, the holy Law of the Spirit of life.

7.7-11 describe this abuse of the Law and so explain, in how far – while it is entirely different from sin in itself – it was yet able to become the 'law of sin', i.e. the law which fosters, increases and reveals human sin, and from which the Gospel has freed us. We learn that sin arises from the Law; from the

F   81

encounter of man with the Law. Man did not know sin, sin was and is foreign to him as long as he does not meet with God's grace in the form of the claim made on him in the shape of the Law. Sin does exist without the Law, but it lurks at the door, it has no occasion (no springboard) from which to become the deed which makes us into God's enemies and so delivers us over to death. It is as yet dead (7.8)! But it comes to life, it finds an opportunity and a springboard, when I encounter the Law. When this encounter takes place, sin arises, becomes active, deceives me and becomes my own sin and consequently the reason of my own damnation. For in opposition to my own desire, and while the Law claims me for God, sin insinuates that I ought to satisfy the Law's demands myself, that I ought to cleanse and justify and sanctify myself. It insinuates that I am too good for the grace offered to me in the Law, that I should refuse it and that instead of the faith demanded by the Law I should present to God my own work, my own religion and my own moral achievement and so make myself worthy before God. It insinuates that God could surely not have said that I cannot be equal to him and that I must be satisfied with his grace, but that he must have meant that I, a second god beside him, should do myself what he wants to do for me. With this insinuation, and because I listen to this insinuation, sin becomes active; that is how it becomes a deed and an event. And in this misunderstanding and abuse of the Law, because of the sin that dwells in me, I become guilty of the prohibited desire, the desire to be as God. I desire this, I desire my own glory before God while I should be content with his glory, while I should serve his glory, so that I may have my glory in his.

And so I come to deserve death. Sin, which enticed and misled me, I myself, by allowing myself to be enticed and misled, have given me over to death. Sin? I myself? Yes indeed. But sin, and because of sin, I myself by means of the Law. Sin which has come to life and has become active because of the Law; I myself as the sinful man who became an active sinner because of my encounter with the Law. The thing which should have guided me to obedience and therefore to life, God's holy commandment, has become my opportunity for disobedience and therefore for death. For this is the disobedience, this is the strong, living sin, compared to which the others are only dummies: the contempt of God's grace, the human effort to lay our hands on that which God wants to be and to do for us, the endeavour to save, safeguard and exalt ourselves, while he wants to be our sole salvation, safeguard and exaltation.

All that God has forbidden has been forbidden because in its origin and its essence it is this one forbidden thing, the act of our hatred of God's grace. While, because we do this forbidden thing, we do everything else. What is at stake in the breaking forth and the revelation of the Gospel in the Law is that this forbidden act is forgiven, effectively forgiven, by the fact that we become different men who can no longer act in this way. This means that (apart from being freed from ourselves) we are freed from the abused prohibition and commandment and that the Law is restored in the form in which God himself gave it to us and meant it. It is for this that Paul, at the end of the chapter, thanks God through our Lord Jesus Christ.

'Did then that which is good (the commandment of God's Law, which according to 7.12 is holy and just) become *death* unto me?' (7.13). That is the second question which Paul is asked and which again he answers with his 'Impossible!' (EVV: 'God forbid!') Admittedly I have been condemned to death by the Law, just as (7.7-12) – the Law provided the opportunity to sin. But there is no more reason here to accuse the Law than there was there. On the contrary there is every reason to accuse sin which pre-eminently proves to be sin (which makes me an inexcusable sinner and delivers me up to death) by taking hold and making use of the Law. Not the good, but sin, by means of the corrupted good, is the cause of my death. While the Law wanted to be my good and to procure life for me, sin

83

enticed me to the wrong belief that I was something different from, something better than a sinner. It made me regard myself as fundamentally good and therefore able to help myself. It enticed me to do the very thing which the Law does not allow in apparent obedience to the Law: to try to make myself guiltless by my own goodness. In this abuse of the commandment given to me sin has become 'exceedingly sinful' and wounded me mortally. For in that way it has robbed me of the righteous verdict of the gracious God, which I had been promised. It brought me up to be a would-be *saint* and so caused my *fall* beyond hope. For it put me in opposition to the God who has pity on the wretched and raises the dead, to whom therefore all human sanctity based on our own skill and strength must be an abomination, to whom as saints of this kind we are lost. 7.14-23 speak of the lost state of the man whom the triumph of sin has made into such a queer saint. The man who moves on this path (7.14) knows that the Law is spiritual, and he knows (7.18) that the good does not dwell in him, i.e. in his flesh. Does he? But how can one then still want to be such a saint? Paul does in fact want to say that, to the extent that one knows what the Law has to say to people who want to be saints of that kind, one *cannot possibly* want to be such a saint (this also applies to the Law abused by sin, because it is and remains *God's* Law and therefore the revelation of the *truth*). For it simply reveals to them their death, inasmuch as it cannot show them anything except that as people who want to be saints *of this kind*, they are in a sense rent in two. *God's Law is not to be mocked.*

1. The Law is spiritual; it undoubtedly demands the complete obedience of the whole man. For this reason anyone who, enticed by sin, presumes to fulfil the Law himself and desires to ensure God's grace for himself by his own efforts, can only learn from the Law (7.14) that he is *carnal*, that he *cannot* hold his own as a man before God, that he *cannot* carry out his intention of becoming righteous and justifying himself before God. Such an intention betrays more than anything else that he

has been *sold under sin* by a transaction that cannot be annulled. In this actual achievement in carrying out that intention he will not be able to recognize what he *wanted* to achieve (7.15). On the contrary, the Law will convince him that he is doing what he has no intention of doing, what he can only detest. But who is he then? The man who has a certain intention? Or the man who does the very thing that he has no intention of doing? Or (7.16) the man who by his loathing of what he does seems to acknowledge the truth of God's Law after all? He certainly has reason to do the latter, but what follows? What he does and achieves (7.17) and of which he disapproves, is not his own doing and achievement but that of sin which dwells in him! *In him!* Is it then possible for him to deny all complicity with this guest in his house, would he perhaps be able to justify himself by his protest against its work? But his protest would obviously be too late to justify him, even if he could deny his complicity, even if he could deny that sin is *his* sin. He may try, but it is certain that he wanted to justify and sanctify himself by his own work and that he must now condemn that work of his as the work of sin.

2. Anyone who is enticed by sin to presume to fulfil God's Law himself, is told by the Law (which holds him entirely responsible, as is his foolish desire) only that good, which he would need to *do* good, does not dwell *in him* (7.18). He is flesh, in his deepest and innermost being he is God's enemy and the object of God's wrath. The *absence* of the second guest corresponds with the *presence* of the first. For we cannot assume that both can dwell under one roof. We must observe that Paul does not deny that this queer saint desires to do what is right: he may very well be a man who sincerely desires, seeks and strives. But Paul's original plan did not merely envisage a desire, but man's justifying and sanctifying fulfilment of it. The desire to do good cannot be treated as an exception if it does not result in the doing of good, any more than the desire not to do evil can be excepted.

And it does not result in the doing of good (7.19). What the

85

Law finds in man, what by the light of the Law which he wanted to fulfil man finds in himself, is the doing of *evil*, in spite of his good will. Any appeal to his good will (7.20) can only confirm that sin dwells in him and does evil in spite of him. Once more: who is he? The man who wills, who desires? The man who does not do what he desires? The man who contradicts his desires by what he does and his actions by what he desires? The fact that he is merely the owner of the house where sin dwells shall certainly not save him. Sin certainly results when anyone plans a systematic justification and sanctification of himself by his own actions.

Verses 21-23 sum up: the queer saint who is led astray by sin and endeavours to put his hands on God's grace is in fact a man rent in two. While he wants to fulfil God's Law by himself, evil is there (7.21). While he rejoices in God's Law (7.22) – if only he would do it in the right way, if only he would not allow himself to be enticed by sin to abuse the Law – he can only discover and observe in himself the unequal and desperate struggle (7.23) between the Law which he had undertaken to fulfil and the law in his members.[1] He can only see the inner necessity of all his human existence as such, which contravenes his intention, however thoroughly and sincerely he may pursue it, which in its quality as the law of sin keeps him a prisoner, whichever way he may turn. Again and again he will abide by this other law. At the end of all his pains and endeavours he will ever and again be what he is and not what he desires to be and to make of himself. But is he not at the same time the man who desires to be something else and who by all these pains and endeavours wants to make something else out of himself? Which of the two is he? One thing is certain. Whichever of the two he may be, he is not the man who achieves that which, all too boldly, he has undertaken! And it is certain that in the split of this double existence between desire and achievement he is a man who is doomed to

[1] So most EVV. Weymouth translates 'faculties'. Literally 'limbs'. *Translator.*

death! For what is death if it is not this split life? The sigh in
7.24 applies to this life which is a living death: 'O wretched
man that I am! Who shall deliver me out of the body of this
death?' Delivery from this disruption? Delivery from this
existence which is but one continuous dissolution of myself?

Man will *not* deliver himself from this existence under the
law of sin and death. Note how the two sections 7.7-12 and
13-23 are dominated by the word 'I'. No sentence beginning
with that word could describe man's liberation. The Christian
'I' too, the Christian 'I' particularly, must and shall admit its
own state of bondage, its disruption. This is shown by the
remarkable verse 25 where the Christian 'I' confesses that Jesus
Christ is its Deliverer. He who confesses Jesus Christ in particular will know that *I* shall never be able to leave sin behind
by myself. *I* shall never leave behind the adulteration of the
Law by sin. *I* shall never leave the existence of that queer
saint who desires to be as God and who must therefore be
dying alive, behind me. I am and live in the flesh, and therefore I am and remain subjected to the law of sin and death
(7.11). There is no line which starts with 'I' and finishes
somewhere with salvation and liberty. But as we showed in
7.1-6 there is the other line, which starts with Jesus Christ, in
which the man who is subject to that law, was killed, not in his
own death but in the death of Jesus Christ. He has been killed
and therefore liberated from himself, to live now for that other
One, who rose from the dead (7.4), to serve the Law of *God*
(7.25) in the new condition of the Spirit (7.6), as a man who has
been liberated and is now fully subordinated to that Other, the
Son of God.

The Gospel as the Establishment of God's Law

THE man who as Adam's child does what Adam does is condemned. All *flesh* is condemned as the human nature in which sin dwells. Above all the *pious*, the *moral* flesh is condemned: the man who bends and breaks God's Law by assuming that he has to justify and sanctify himself before God. He especially is condemned by the Law of God which he has bent and broken, because even so it does not cease to be true and effective. In rejecting God's grace (to which the Law tells him to cleave), in order to work out his own salvation instead, by fulfilling the letter of the Law (7.6), he *has* already been condemned and can now only die, though he is living.

But 8.1 says that there is no condemnation for those who 'are in Christ Jesus'. The whole of Chapter 8 will teach us how the condemnation of man has been abrogated. God meets that bending and breaking of his Law by establishing it anew and more than ever as his Law in Jesus Christ, by obtaining for it due respect and observance through Jesus Christ and thereby making his grace triumphant with and *for* everyone who believes in Jesus Christ. He therefore does not only liberate those who believe in Jesus Christ from the Law of sin and death but he also – as we shall hear in due course – positively sets them free for a life in obedience (8.12-16), hope (8.17-27) and innocence (8.28-39), in a word: for a life in the *Spirit*, under his will of *grace*. This is the fourth explanation of the thesis in 1.16 concerning God's *almighty work of salvation* for everyone who believes, or of that in 1.17 that he who is righteous through his

88

faith shall *live* because of that faith. This fourth and final explanation declares that with the revelation of the Gospel of Jesus Christ God establishes his Law by giving *his Spirit* to those who believe in Jesus Christ and, with the Spirit, already *here* and *now* that righteous, innocent and blessed life which as such has the promise of being life eternal. The justification of believers is authenticated and the reconciliation, sanctification and liberation of man is completed in the establishment of God's Law, in the dominion of his Spirit.

The fundamental point is made in 8.1-11. 8.1-2, in the first place, confirm 7.1-6. The condemnation of man by the Law of sin and death does not affect those who are in Christ Jesus, because as such they have been *released, liberated* from that Law. They have not set themselves free from it. Any effort to liberate themselves could only result in what 7.3 has described, harshly enough, as adultery. In the prison of that Law the last word can always only be the hopeless sigh of 7.24: 'O wretched man that I am!' Things beginning with 'I' do not lead to liberation and will never be real, eternal life. But the 'Law of the Spirit of life' has liberated those who are in Christ Jesus. To 'be in Christ Jesus' is evidently the same as to be subject to this entirely different Law. And both together clearly point to that entirely new aspect, indeed that entirely new reality of human life, to which reference was made in 7.1, and which will now be discussed at length. It is there in the fact that man need no longer start with 'I', with himself, but is allowed to start with Jesus Christ because Jesus Christ has made a fresh start with him. 'To be in Christ Jesus' means that he is a man to whom this has happened. And this new reality consists in the fact that where a man is allowed to start with Jesus Christ instead of with 'I' – because Jesus Christ has made a fresh start with him – the Law first of all liberates *itself* from abuse by sin. First of all the Law *itself* breaks 'through' that perverted form of a law of sin and death, and shows itself in its true form as the Spirit which moves this man to seek

89

God's grace. In so doing it also liberates this *man* from this perverted form of the law and from the distress which in that form it must cause him, and so too it makes this man break through to the path of life, hope and innocence.

We read in 8.3 that this establishment of the Law as something that liberates has once and for all been achieved by what God brought about in Jesus Christ. That which was not possible to the Law in its perverted form, in its infirmity, because of sin which dwells in our flesh, God has made not only possible but real by sending his Son. God has done this by really sending his eternal Son, really to us, by really making him not merely similar to but the same as *us*, as this flesh of ours, inhabited and dominated by sin. God has made him the same as us 'for the sake of sin', i.e. to *meet* sin in the place where it dwells and rules, and there to condemn, judge and remove it, to break its dominion, to expose its deceit and to do away with its consequences.

That is what Jesus Christ has done, he who was without sin humbled himself in our stead as a sinner before God. He suffered the punishment of death due to us and in that way rendered to God the obedience which we deny him, in that way he accepted in our stead God's grace which we always want to decline. In him (8.4) we have been put to death as the sinners which we were and are, and are therefore dead as regards the law of sin and death to which as sinners we were and still are subjected. And with him we now live another life, a new life. In him God's Law stands *before* us and powerfully *over* us in its pure and true form: a single irresistible offer and command of God's grace to us who have been put to death with him and now live with him. To begin with him – because he has made a beginning with us – 'to be in Christ' simply means to be *bound* by the pure and true Law of God established and made effective in him; to be *compelled* and *allowed* to accept the offer of God's grace and to be obedient to the command of God's grace, which has appeared in him; as men who were dead and who have been brought to life by him. That is 'to walk after the Spirit and no longer after the flesh'. The *fulfilment* of the Law is therefore achieved in those who walk after the Spirit. For 'to walk after the Spirit' is nothing but to become *obedient* to God's *grace* which has appeared with compelling power in Jesus Christ. In all that follows and in the whole of this chapter we must remember that by the 'Spirit' Paul means nothing but the validity and the power of the Law of grace established by the sending of the Son of God over those who believe in him, because he has died and risen for them.

Their flesh is still there, their human nature in which sin dwells, in which no good thing dwells. They still are and have an ego, the 'I' from which there is no way to liberation and life. There still exists in them that queer saint who allows himself to be deceived by sin through the Law and for whom the law of sin must ever become the law of death. They still know only too well what life in disruption is like. But they no longer *walk* after the flesh but after the Spirit (8.4). They 'are' not in the flesh but in the Spirit (8.5, 9). They do not have the disposition, the structure and the inclination of the flesh but of the Spirit. But this means that they are not once more torn *between* the Spirit and the flesh. For their part, as they already belong to the Spirit, they have *decided* for the Spirit and against the flesh. They have turned their faces to the Spirit as the power of the Law of grace, and they have turned their backs on the flesh as their existence dominated by sin and therefore disrupted. About the flesh no more can be said than that it is still there, a possibility which as such has not yet been abolished, a constant invitation to walk in the flesh and a constant danger of walking in it, of living in it, of doing what accords with its disposition, structure and inclination. And according to Chapter 7 that would mean again to hate and reject God's grace, once more to want to justify and sanctify oneself. That is what the flesh always wants to do. It is unwilling to be subject to God's Law, it cannot be, or it would not be the flesh; our human nature as determined and characterized by Adam's sin (8.7).

The fulfilment of the intentions *of the flesh* can only end in death, and what we do in pursuance of *its* intentions, will always be subjected to death (8.6). For 'they that are in the flesh cannot please God' (8.8): 'I' cannot please God – as I am and know myself – here and now! But then 'I' – as this ego – have no actual meaning any more, because I 'am in Christ Jesus' because the Law of God which he has established and made strong has power over me. I would not be subject to that Law, I would not belong to Jesus Christ, if I did not have his Spirit, if his Spirit which is the Spirit of God did not dwell in me (8.9), if Christ himself were not in me and had not in my stead assumed dominion over me and responsibility for me. Consequently the question of what is applicable to me and what dominates me, and therefore also the question of who I am has been decided against the flesh that exists and works behind me. It has not been decided by me but by the fact that in Jesus Christ God's Law has been established for me and over me and cannot be invalidated. That Law ties me to God's grace, and therefore I have become a stranger to the flesh and its desires, however near they may be to me. I have been delivered from death which is its inevitable result and have been brought to peace and therefore to life (8.6).

I? After all? Yes: this we learn in 8.10-11. The last and greatest miracle, for which we are heading, thanks to the establishment of God's Law, thanks to the decision for the Spirit and against the flesh is first, that the 'body', this 'I' this human personality which I am, will admittedly have to die because of sin, as it has already happened to me in the death of Jesus Christ at Golgotha, long before the hour of death for which I am making now. Secondly, my only life is the Spirit of God and of Jesus Christ, who has delivered me from that body (7.24), who has transferred me into the righteousness of a man who only desires to live by grace. Thirdly now this same Spirit, the Spirit of the God who raised Jesus from the dead, because he has been given to me, because he dwells in me, does not abandon 'my body' to death. He does not abandon me, this 'I', this human personality, all that has been marked out for death and subjected to death. He will make me to live with Jesus, cleansed from the nature of flesh, as the ego, the character and the person of the man whom God has loved from eternity – conformed to the body of the risen and exalted Jesus. God takes nothing from us that he does not intend to restore to us in a redeemed form – that means in an infinitely better form. He does not take our 'I' without restoring it to us in Jesus Christ. But he has to take it from us before he can restore it to us redeemed. We must and may therefore be content here and now to live in the Spirit of God and Jesus Christ, but to see our bodies, ourselves hastening towards death, comforted in advance because the bitterness of death has already been suffered and conquered on the cross of Golgotha. And over all graves there is the promise that by the same Spirit we ourselves, our bodies, shall live forever.

It is certainly reasonable and justified to regard at least 8.12-16, the first and shortest of the expositions which now follow, as a description of the *obedience* which is characteristic of the life of those who 'are in Christ Jesus'. What but their obedience could correspond so closely with the establishment of God's Law in which they have obtained a share? To what purpose have they been reconciled with God (Chapter 5), sanctified (Chapter 6) and liberated from the abused Law (Chapter 7) if not to be obedient? In a wider sense the *whole* of Chapter 8 could very well be regarded as one description of the obedience of those whose Law is the Spirit of God. But since this is discussed more especially in 8.12-16, we must say right away as regards 8.12 that there is now no longer any question of an obedience which those who are in Christ Jesus are *obliged* to render, which they *must* and *shall* render. Admittedly in 6.16, 17, 22; 7.6 their life was called a 'service', but even there it was in close connection with 'liberty' and the 'Spirit'.

We shall meet the idea of service again in the Epistle to the Romans (e.g. in 12.11 and 14.18). Paul generally makes much of it and constantly refers to himself as a minister, a servant, a slave of Jesus Christ. This passage is quite unambiguous about the way in which Christian service should not be understood. The Spirit of obedience to God's Law is certainly no slavish spirit. It is not a spirit of wage-slavery; it is not the spirit of a debtor, in which we would have reason to be afraid – in the way that we had to be afraid of God when we bent and broke his Law and wanted to justify ourselves (8.17). We are not God's debtors having to raise interest for him in fear and embarrassment, or perhaps even the whole borrowed capital sum, with the intention of eventually facing him triumphantly. It was just that attitude which was our life after the flesh.

This intention was the plan – prohibited, impracticable and fatal – of sin, which inhabited and dominated our flesh. And in that attitude we were of a truth indebted and subject to the flesh and not to God (or only to the flesh's idea of God!). The indebtedness and obligation from which those who are in Christ Jesus have been set free (8.12) is that they should not enter into that same sad and barren relationship to God – particularly as regards God this relationship is simply impossible. On the strength of what has been done for them in Jesus Christ, in the power of the Spirit they are to kill, ignore and relinquish all the 'practices' ('deeds', EVV: 8.13) which the 'body', which 'I' would still continue to desire they are to deny this relationship persistently by a genuine obedience to God's Law. Those who are led, moved and drawn by the Spirit of God (8.14) – and this is the essence of being in Christ Jesus – do not serve him because as his debtors they are simply obliged to and certainly not because they have the debtor's ideal of making themselves free of him. On the contrary – and this is their life in Jesus Christ the Son of God – they are God's sons who do his will because he is their father, because they are his sons. Thanks to the Spirit of God which as the Spirit of Jesus Christ is the Spirit of sonship, they have, in their own freedom, out of themselves no choice or possibility but to do his will (8.15). But they fulfil his will by crying to him. From

94

and in the depth of the distress of their human existence they cry to him, but no longer 'O wretched man that I am' but 'Abba, Father'. They cry to him as prodigal sons, lost children, but in their very state of lostness they have been told to call him Father, to cleave to him as the 'Father of mercy' and the 'God of all consolation' (II Cor. 1.3) – as Jesus did in fact instruct his people to do! In their very state of lostness they cannot help doing the one good work of *crying* out in this way and so performing the one act of *obedience* demanded by the Law. Or could they help obeying grace by such crying out, could they have any inclination to lapse into the 'practices' of a relationship with God which could never be without fear, which could only end in death, which could only blaspheme the name of God?

How else is it possible for this to happen again and again? Under the very pressure of this constant threat and danger, the Spirit of God will by his testimony assist their weak spirit, which ever knows that it is weak. From the established Law of God, from the cross at Golgotha, where their destiny was decided, they shall hear again and again that we are God's children (8.16)! We have no power to do any good by ourselves. We, whose flesh is inhabited and dominated by sin. We who are selfish, rebellious and useless servants, are yet God's children! This testimony, the testimony of the Holy Spirit is certainly needed before our own unholy spirit, under his impact and impulse, also testifies to this. We must be told, so that we can tell ourselves that we are God's children! And it cannot fail to happen that from this source we are told again and again, and that consequently we may tell ourselves: we are God's children!

And again, it cannot fail to happen that we may and must enter into the good work of obedience which consists in our crying out 'Abba! Father!' We must observe that particularly at this culminating point of the Epistle to the Romans there is no mention of any other work of obedience of God's children. The purpose of our reconciliation with God, our sanctification for God and our liberation from the law of sin and death is that this work should be done. By doing this work we follow the guiding and drawing of the Spirit and prove that we are no longer debtors to the flesh. It is obvious that no other work of obedience can or shall be added to this. All acts of obedience ought obviously to be included in it. They ought to arise from it and in all circumstances they ought to have their root and archetype, their first and their last condition in it. To those who are in Christ Jesus it appears that nothing is allowed which is not in tune with this crying out of God's children to their Father. And it appears that they have been allowed all that they need as such children crying out to their Father. Both that which is prohibited and that which is commanded can and does include many things – the last chapters of the Epistle can give us some impression of that. But because it is the Law of his grace, the fulfilment of God's Law (8.4) will primarily and finally always consist in that which these verses define as *the* gift of the Spirit. A Christian either replies to the testimony of the Spirit in the way described in 8.15, or he does not reply at all – which would mean that he is not yet or is no longer a Christian.

In the large central section, 8.17-27,[1] the point of view that obedience is the characteristic quality of life under God's Law is neither abandoned nor substantially changed. We only have to look at 8.23, 26 to realize that. But another point of view becomes paramount: that life under God's Law as the life in obedience is a life in *hope*. I mean, it is life in the certain and strong expectation, which therefore fills and dominates the present, of the life of those who are in Christ Jesus, already created and founded by the Spirit. We have already learned, in 8.10-11, that this life is on its way to consummation in such a revelation, to the bringing to life again of our bodies that are here and now subjected to death, the restoration of that which now as our 'ego' can only perish so that the Spirit may live.

The same perspective is viewed once more in 8.17. Conse-

---

[1] Cf. *KD*, IV, 2, p. 367f, ET, p. 329f.

quently we now meet with the actual counterpart of the picture of man as subjected to the law of sin and death which was so vividly described in 7.7-23. The man who has been liberated from that law, even the man whom the Spirit has made subject to the Law of God, lives in the victorious decision for the Spirit and against the flesh (8.1-11) in the obedience of God's children (8.12-16). Yet he is living here and now, where the flesh is at any rate still in the background, where sin, dwelling in the flesh and dominating it is still an invitation, a temptation, a danger. That we are living here and now means that we are living where the cross of Christ does not only shed the *light* which it spreads as the cross of the risen One.

It also casts its *shadow* (of death) across our whole human condition. This condition has been judged and put to death on the cross of the Son of God; now it can only learn, and must in fact learn, that it has been judged and killed there. Its further existence can only be temporary. It will pass away and thus it will confirm, will inevitably have to confirm, this death. Those who are in Christ Jesus, inasmuch as they live here and now, also live in the shadow of death, under its promise, but also under its inexorable fatality. As truly as they are God's children (8.17) they are also God's heirs, i.e. they have expectations of sharing in what belongs to God and is characteristically his own: the glory of his life, into which Christ has already been assumed and into which they expect to be assumed with him as surely as their only future is in him who died for them and in whom they too have died. Their present, which precedes that future with him, can obviously only be one that is determined by his suffering. 'Still living' after his death certainly means on the one hand *no longer* having *to be afraid* of our own death because it has already taken place in him, because he has already tasted and suffered its bitterness to the very end, so that we no longer have to endure it. On the other hand 'still living' after his death equally certainly means *still* being subject to the *temptation* which he experienced before his death, in Gethsemane – not without him, with him, but even so with him in

G   97

temptation, in the place where he stood as the humiliated Son of God. We can gather from 5.3-4, but we must realize particularly from the whole of the remainder of Chapter 8, that Paul considers the place of temptation as an *excellent* place, a place full of promise where we can suffer things that are evil only for the time being, only very limited evil. Let us rejoice in standing at that place, said 5.3-4. How could it be otherwise, since we are not standing there alone but with Christ: with him, who from that place entered into God's glory. Therefore there follows no word of complaint that our life after the death of Jesus Christ is such that it can only develop in the shadow of his death, that it can consist only in having to suffer with him.

How can it be otherwise, since we are allowed to be under God's Law? For this means (8.18) that the relationship between what we have to suffer in our present place and the glory that shall be revealed in us is such that there is no room left for any complaining on our part. The suffering can never be regarded as a harsh obligation and we can only speak of the *hope* in which it is actually suffered by those who are in Christ Jesus. The reason is that the shadow falling on them from the cross of Golgotha can only be the herald of the glory that awaits them. We ought to bear in mind that this has nothing to do with idealism or optimism. Paul regards that which is to be suffered as an inevitable effect of the death of Christ (in which truly an end has been made of all idealism and optimism): for this reason, and only for this reason, he can see the sufferings of this time far outweighed by the glory to come. He sees all things – really all – as they are and not as he might like to see them. And for Paul the resurrection of Jesus Christ which followed his death on Golgotha does not merely take the first place among all things but the all-controlling place from which he can regard the temptation of Jesus Christ before his death and our own only as an upward beat that cannot last but is only heard for a moment to fade away in what follows.

In the following passage it is made abundantly clear that Paul also sees all other things as they are, in the world as well as among the Christians. He says in 8.19-22 that those who are in Christ Jesus are not alone in their expectation of the coming glory of God which will change all things, but that they are surrounded by the whole creation which as such is heading for the same renewal. On the other hand he says in 8.23 that the groaning for redemption is not only the concern of the unredeemed world outside us, but also and in the first place the concern of the Christians. The word 'creation', used four times in 8.19-23, means according to NT usage in the first place and above all *man* in general, *mankind*, which has not yet heard the Gospel but which is yet to hear it. In a wider sense it includes *all that has been created*, the animals and inanimate nature that surrounds man and his history which according to the biblical view of the world was created for the sake of man, to be dominated by man. For that very reason we shall have to apply what Paul says in the first place to man as the centre of God's creation.

What Paul says about creation in its totality becomes manifest in mankind: that – whether it knows this or not – mankind is in a state of longing expectation because it is subjected to vanity, because it is 'in bondage of corruption', that is to say because all its works and enterprises, its entire life in all its impulses and movements ever and again end in dust and oblivion; because all the conservation of energy and matter, because all the continuity of its development does not alter the fact that all its growth can never lead to any subsistence or permanence but only, again and again, to annihilation and non-existence – very much against its will, for it would manifestly rather live and not die, but with all its life it can do nothing else but die. In its loathing for the necessity of perishing to which it has been subjected, creation – we repeat, whether it knows this or not – is the *longing and groaning* creation, according to 8.22 travailing in pain.

But what about the necessity of passing away to which it is subjected? Who has subjected man, and with him the whole creation, to vanity (8.20)? There seems to me to be no doubt that here as well, Paul is simply thinking of Jesus Christ who in his death, as we have heard again and again, has made an end of man, has pronounced and executed his verdict. Along with man the whole world suffers from the fact that this has happened. At Golgotha the final word has been spoken concerning man and his whole world, and therefore there is for man and his world no prospect of subsistence and permanence. That is why things here and now only arise and exist for a while, to be destroyed. That is why as far as the eye can reach there is only dying life. That is why here and now creation in all its glory can only be a groaning creation, 'in service of vanities, still oppressing us so sore, even though our spirit sometimes seeks a better shore'. But since Jesus Christ subjected us, it is a subjection 'in hope' (8.20). The promise given to those who are God's children in Jesus Christ, shows *what* man and with him all creation is groaning for, *what* they lack, *what* is the liberty corresponding to that subjection and vanity. For just as there is no other subjection except to God's judgment in the death of Jesus Christ, so there is no other liberty than the liberty of his glory, to which the children of God are looking forward as his heirs. Wherever and however men groan for liberty they do not do so in vain. Because that judgment applies to the whole world, the whole world has been given this future, the whole world has been promised this answer to its groaning: this new birth as the fruit of its travails: 'the creation itself shall be delivered from the bondage of corruption into the liberty of the glory of the children of God' (8.21). It therefore waits with the children of God for the revelation of the glory: with their future God's children are a guarantee for the future which all men and all things have before them (8.19). But just as the world shares in their hope, so they have to share in the groaning which permeates the whole world (8.23): not in spite of the fact that they already have the 'first fruits of the Spirit' but because of it, because in the Spirit they already have the beginning of the future glory: they already share in the blessing of God's Law as the 'Spirit of life' (8.2). While according to the testimony of the Spirit to their spirit they already are God's children (8.16), the revelation, the unveiling of what they are, the time when their right and inheritance as sons comes into effect is yet in the future. We may here compare I John 3.1f: 'Behold what manner of love the Father has bestowed on us that we should be called children of God, and such we are . . . Beloved, already now we are children of God and it has not yet been made manifest, what we shall be. But we do know that when it shall be manifested, we shall be like him.' Like him: in the 'redemption of our body', in the restoration of the 'I', the ego that can here and now only perish, that can here and now only face the life of the Spirit, which is God's Spirit and not our own, as something else, something foreign.

In view of that decay God's children also share in the longing expectation of all creation. They also groan, but not without consolation. How can they be unconsoled, when already here and now they have the Spirit? But they do groan. They know of the consummation but they do not yet have it. 'In hope we were saved' (8.24). Both words should receive equal emphasis. Nothing needs to be added to our salvation, which has taken place in Jesus Christ. 'It is finished' (John 19.30).

What is lacking is that the finished work, inasmuch as it also includes our glorification, is as yet *hidden*, is as yet *not visible*. The expected consummation exists only in his revelation (8.18, 19). But the hope is concerned with that very revelation – and so is faith inasmuch as it is hope, as was Abraham's faith (4.18ff). Hope is directed towards the fulfilment of the divine promise, in the possession of which we may already live here and now. Faith is hope inasmuch as it knows the promise and cleaves to it, although it cannot yet see its fulfilment; the future, promised by God, consisting in the redemption of our body, in our life in the glory of the risen Christ. Faith is hope inasmuch as we are allowed to share with him the weakness, the suffering and the temptation of the humiliated Son of God, because his future in glory is ours as well.

Faith is hope inasmuch as it consists in the patience (8.25), the endurance and the steadfastness, with which, groaning and nevertheless comforted, we may wait for the fulfilment of the promise. That patience has been made necessary; it has also been made easy. Jesus Christ himself is our hope; we need no longer wait for anything save the revelation of that which he has already finished, for our waiting as such is already full of the presence of that for which we are waiting. On the strength of the established Law of God that has been made really easy for us, Paul now gives (8.26-27) an explanation analogous to that in 8.16. Those who are in Christ Jesus are *not* left to their own strength to be patient, to the ardour and enthusiasm of their hope. But while they are in the midst, and, like the rest of the world in the service of decay, and therefore together with all creation cannot stop groaning, the Spirit helps their infirmity.

How? The important thing about continuing in hope, in patient expectation, is for us to continue, to carry on in that work of calling on God, of crying 'Abba, Father!' (8.15), in which grace is accepted as grace and the Law is fulfilled. And the Spirit helps us in the doing of that work; yea, the Spirit himself makes intercession for us. For how can we know what proper prayer is, how should he be in a position to pray this 'Abba, Father' in the right way as the one saving prayer? How could we have understood that grace is grace, if we did not shrink from this work in particular? Who can pray in this fashion? Who can speak to God in such a way that he pleases God with these words, and be heard by him? And now Paul says that in this very decisive act God himself makes intercession on our behalf. He says that he makes himself our advocate with himself, that he utters for us that ineffable groaning, so that he will surely hear what we ourselves could not have told him, so that he will accept what he himself has to offer. That is what has supremely and finally, in the establishment of the Law, become a reality for those who are in Christ Jesus. That is why they will not give up hope, even if they want to. It is the secret of their patience. In their joyless and powerless groaning God hears the voice of his own Son and this turns their groaning into the worship that pleases him, and turns it for them into that comforted groaning that prevents them from every losing hope.

The last part of Chapter 8, vv. 28-39,[1] describes life under God's Law as a life in *innocence*. We derive this concept especially from vv. 31-39. There the question is formally raised: who could witness against those who are in Christ Jesus, who could reproach them, accuse them? The answer is given that no one can do this, that this can on no account be done. For the One who could be against them and speak against them, the only One in a position to pronounce them guilty, does the opposite. He is for them and speaks for them. Because he does so – the One who is the source and the measure of all righteousness, who is the eternal Judge – therefore they are innocent.

We have already heard in 8.26-27: in the midst of the world – which in the shadow of the cross can only perish, and as belonging to which they too must perish – they have strength for that hope which according to 5.5 does not put to shame, in the fact that the Spirit makes intercession for them, speaks for them so that in their weak and defective prayers God hears the voice of his own Son, in whom he is well pleased, so that this pleasure benefits them too, so that he hears them as his children when from the depths they cry unto him (8.15): 'Abba, Father!' The Spirit is God's grace triumphant in their faith over their whole bondage to sin and death. This Spirit is the counsel for the defence, who acquits them because he is also their Law and their Judge. And we already heard in 8.1: 'There is therefore no condemnation to them that are in Christ Jesus.' That is the message which is now taken up again at the end of the chapter.

When it says in 8.28 that to them that love God all things work together for good, 'all things' should be understood to refer to all that which, whether as a temporal-historical experience (8.35) or as a spiritual-supernatural influence (8.38), might

[1] Cf. *KD*, IV, 2, p. 308f, ET, pp. 278f.

have the power to rob the Christian – who after all is not exempt from such experience and influences – of the liberty of the innocence in which he stands before God. Why do they in fact not have that power? Because, it says in 8.35 and 39, none of those possibilities are by any means sufficient to separate them from the love of God – 8.35 calls it the love of Christ, 8.39 the love of God in Jesus Christ our Lord – which according to 5.5 was poured out into their hearts. None of these possibilities is sufficient to tear that love from their hearts, so that they would once more be left without love – and therefore to themselves. Paul is speaking of the love that God shows us by allowing us to love him again as his children because of his own Son. Where that love is present – and it is and remains in those who are in Christ Jesus – all these dangers are no dangers but helps (8.28), there any temptation that might threaten from those possibilities can only serve to confirm and to strengthen men in obedience and in hope, therefore in innocence and consequently in the liberty of God's children. This is the good for which all things work together to them.

To them that love God! Paul now makes it clear once more that in the context of the Gospel this love cannot mean that men have chosen, prepared and acquired for themselves the fact that they have turned towards God and their surrender to him, as if they had any idea what to do about God, as if they had any inclination or ability towards God. Paul is speaking of the living power of the Spirit, of the Law of life established at Golgotha. Those who love God are the ones whom God from all eternity, according to his free will, has destined and in due time called to such love. He has on their behalf dealt with them (8.29-30). He knew about them and by knowing and thinking about them he gave them their purpose – both in advance, i.e. by himself, in the power of his almighty mercy which existed before they were, yea, before the world was (Eph. 1.4). While they were yet deaf he called them by his word, while they were yet ungodly he told them, in the hearing of the whole celestial and earthly creation, that they were righteous, while they were yet subject to temptation he clothed them with his own glory.

Note how Paul describes all this in the past tense, as an historical, indeed pre-historical, eternal fact. Let the bondage of sin and death be as it may! Let the fear in which, subjected to the law of sin and death, they doubt the sufficiency of God's grace and let the pride which would ever want to substitute their own work for God's grace be as great as it may! That is the fact they have behind them. That is the origin of their existence, as the new, real birth which they received through God's word and will. They have the fact behind them that they are twice born men and this is the power of God's Law over them. When they love God, the work of the Spirit is being done, because this love happens without and against them and only so for them and really and properly to them. So it becomes their own love, poured out in their hearts, the love of their own hearts, that is why it can subsequently be said that no one and nothing can separate them from it. It is a matter of the superior power of God's own love, when men love him so that all temptation can only help them to stand and walk before him the more innocently.

In 8.29 Paul substantiates this by describing the eternal fore-ordination, the predestination, the execution of which brings about the calling, justification and glorification of man, in time in the following terms: God has from eternity conformed them to his own image, i.e. – for this is the image of God (Col. 1.15) – to the form of his own Son. From eternity he has thought of them as he has from eternity thought of his own Son, and so he has given them their purpose for their temporal existence. By the love with which God loves his own Son they have been destined to be his children and therefore to love him in return. Therefore that love has superior power: without them, against them and so for them, so in them. Therefore it is impossible to separate them from that love. Therefore all temptation can only be a help.

Therefore – we now arrive at the main part in 8.31ff – they are not accused in God's sight. They are not accused, however much accusation may be raised against them. 'If God is for us, who can be against us?' It would be self-willed stubbornness if those who are in Christ Jesus were still to maintain that any-one or anything was against them, that their innocence was not certain, that once more they might have to have recourse to fear and pride. Because they love God it is certain whence they have come and therefore also whither they are going. God is for them. For that, according to 8.29-30, is the secret of their love. God is for them. For he has not spared his own Son – the same for whose sake he has from everlasting thought of them as his beloved children – in him he has not spared him-self, he has not regarded himself as too precious.

In him God has 'delivered himself up' so that their eternal predestination should be accomplished and fulfilled. Delivered him up – the expression is the same as that used in 1.24, 26, 28 for the divine delivering up of men to their self-chosen fate – to the infamy of human sin and human death: for their sake, so that this infamy should be taken away from them and no longer be theirs. They stand and live under the law of this event. How then should they not be innocent? How then should they not have been given and ever again be given everything that can show and prove their innocence? For (8.34): who will, who can, who shall accuse them? They have that origin. They are God's elect. Their eternal election has in the midst of time at Golgotha become a fact for all ages. They have for a Judge the One who has already justified them and as whose final word they may forever hear this verdict.

Who damns, who condemns, who rejects these men? Paul does not deny – how could he? – that there is such a damnation, condemnation and rejection of man – of these men too – that they have deserved it a thousand times and that they are hope-lessly subjected to it. But who executes it? The answer is that Jesus Christ executes it. He has executed it once and for all for us and thus also on us – by bearing it himself and dying as its bearer. The One who has also risen, who is on the right hand of God, through whom God governs and judges the world

– Paul uses the same expression as in 8.27 for the Spirit – makes intercession for us. In him God is therefore not against us but for us. For his sake we have our just damnation, condemnation and rejection behind us and no longer before us. Since that is so, it would be self-willed stubbornness for those who are in him not to believe in their own innocence, in their liberty as God's children – if they were not to take this gift completely seriously. If they did not believe in this liberty of theirs they would not believe in God.

Those who love God! In 8.35ff Paul returns once more to this destiny of theirs, to emphasize particularly that it cannot be lost. It does not belong to the characteristics of man; because they are created, these can and will one day disappear, as creation will decay, owing to the temptation both from heaven and from earth, which can and which does in fact every day befall even the Christian. There is no one and nothing that can separate them from the love of Christ. Verses 35-37 in the first place remind us – it is the only time this is done in the Epistle to. the Romans – that the Christians of Paul's day, evidently those in Rome as well, are living under persecution. This is the greatest possible earthly temptation. Under persecution, the manifest demonstration of their failure in the world and of their own share in its corruptibility (8.19ff) they are in danger of losing their innocence, of losing sight of the Law of life under which they live, of giving to natural fear and natural pride a place to which these are not entitled. Persecution might drive Christians away from Christ, rob them of the Spirit and take the love of God away from them. Paul does not answer that this must not happen and that they must guard against it; he says that this cannot happen. Proof of that is no longer needed, but anyone who wants to look for one can find it in the quotation from Ps. 44: 'For thy sake we are killed all the day long, we are counted as sheep for the slaughter.' 'For thy sake'; they are persecuted just because of their relation with Jesus Christ and their union with him, just because they live under the Law of God as it was established at Golgotha – in the same way as all the suffering of the whole creation is secretly the radiation of the suffering of the Son of God and therefore a suffering in hope.

But temptation in fellowship and union with the temptation which Jesus Christ himself suffered and bore cannot separate from him; it can only make stronger the relation and the union and therefore also the love. 'In all these things we are more than conquerors' – not because of our courage and stamina but 'because of him who loved us' with that everlasting love, realised and revealed in the midst of time, which could not possibly shake but only confirm and strengthen the persecuted in their state of innocence, and which shows their limits to all fear descending upon us and to all pride rising in us. Behind and above the earthly temptation and hidden in it lurks the greater and more dangerous temptation from the invisible heavenly powers of this world.

8.38-39 speak of these: death, life, angels, principalities, things present, things to come, powers, height, depth. We must take into account that Paul has here visualized a whole upsurge of spiritual realities, a whole agitated sea of hidden rebellion of which the persecution of the Christians is merely a symptom. He has visualized them not abstractly but in very personal forms, these 'gods many and lords many' (I Cor. 8.5), these 'rulers of this world' (I Cor. 2.6ff), who were ultimately and fundamentally those who crucified the Lord of glory because they did not know the wisdom of God. Of them too Paul says that they shall not be able to separate us from the love of God. This is so for one reason – 8.39 only mentions this in passing – because, even with all their power with all its possibilities, they are only creatures, only 'so-called gods' (I Cor. 8.5). Even their tumult can only bind Christians more closely to him against whom that tumult is really aimed – it has already been silenced and overcome by him against whom it is actually aimed. Everything that the Christians can experience from that quarter is simply the painful consequences of what these powers have for so long tried in vain to do to him. Especially in this their most evil work they were in no way able to act as gods and lords in their own right but ultimately only as servants of the One who by the cross that they erected has brought to light the innocence of those who believe, in such a manner that they are now too late if they still want to take it from them. 8.1 stands. There is therefore no condemnation to them that are in Christ Jesus! No condemnation – that is the ultimate gladness of the glad tidings of the Gospel.

The Gospel among the Jews[1]

IT is evident that in these chapters we are dealing with a second, comparatively independent part of the Epistle. They cannot be concerned any more with a further explanation of the thesis in 1.16 on the Gospel as God's almighty work of salvation for everyone who believes, and consequently they cannot be simply a continuation of the argument in 1.18–8.39. What is true of these chapters applies also to the subsequent, the final part of the whole work, in Chapters 12-16. All that needs saying about that work of salvation, about the life that has been promised in the Gospel to the man who is righteous through his faith, has been said in what precedes. What is now left is the question: what does it mean when the Gospel so described – the Gospel as the divine justification of the believer, as man's reconciliation with God, as his sanctification and liberation, as the establishment of God's Law – meets with disobedience and when it meets with obedience?

What it means when the Gospel meets with obedience Paul set forth in Chapters 12-15, not in the form of a theory but strikingly (how else is it possible to speak of obedience?) in the form of a series of definite exhortations and instructions. But it is equally striking that he does not deal with the problem of disobedience to the Gospel in the form of a corresponding series of accusations and impeachments, nor in the form of a penitential sermon. On the contrary he deals with it by means of a theory, in the best sense of the word, i.e. in the form of an

---

[1] For these three chapters cf. *KD*, II, 2, pp. 222f, 235f, 264f, 294f (ET pp. 202f, 213f, 240f, 267f).

adoring and glorifying contemplation of God's work and way –
these will prove true and are finally triumphant even where
they meet with disobedience of that very God of whom the
Gospel speaks.

If we are inclined to wonder at that, we ought to ask whether
anything else can be expected from the man who has understood
and interpreted the Gospel itself as such, in the way it was done
in Chapter 8. Can anything be expected except that he will
have God's work and way as his only theme, especially as far as
this disobedience to the Gospel is concerned, and that he will
consider and interpret even this disobedience as being *a priori*
and ultimately completely outstripped and eclipsed by his
theme. The last thing we heard was that those who are in
Christ Jesus cannot be separated from God's love. Surely the
man who has dared to say this about himself will have to prove
the truth of these words by the fact that even the sight of the
disobedience which meets the Gospel, does not make him perplexed about his love of God, but can only stimulate him to
praise and worship God. He will prove the truth of his words
by not making his treatment of the problem a complaint about
the bad character of man, but fashioning it into a glorification
of God and his character. That is what Paul has done in these
chapters.

We can ascertain at the end of Chapter 11 what Paul's aim is.
'God has consigned all men to disobedience, that he might have
mercy upon all' (11.32). 'For of him and through him and
unto him are all things' (11.36). In view of all that has gone
before it is certainly not possible to say that here he does not
take the problem of disobedience seriously. But in these verses
as well as in the whole of these chapters he takes it seriously
by taking *God* seriously – the God of whom the *Gospel* speaks
– and giving to him and consequently not to disobedient man
the honour of the final word.

If we look carefully we can already gather from the introduction in 9.1-5, the intention and the result of Paul's discussion

in these chapters of the problem of disobedience to the Gospel. We learn the following from these verses:

1. This problem is to Paul simply identical with the problem of the disobedience of Israel, of the large majority of Israel which declines the Gospel even after the resurrection of Jesus Christ, even after the pouring out of the Holy Spirit. Why Israel in particular? Because, we read in 9.4-5, to a certain extent Israel and the Gospel naturally and fundamentally belong together. Israel as such has already been adopted by God as a son. The glory of God dwells in its midst. God has made his covenant with Israel and again and again renewed it. It has the Law, the worship by sacrifices, the promises and the fathers from its beginnings to this day. In all this Israel has Jesus Christ himself, who according to the flesh was to arise from Israel and did in fact do so: he who is at the same time God himself, who is and reigns over and above all. For these reasons salvation has come to the Jews and from the Jews to the world. God's grace is that grace which was directed towards the Jews, and only through the Jews to the Gentiles too. Therefore Israel is the place where it is decided what disobedience to the Gospel actually is. The full original presence of God's grace is needed for the realisation and the revelation of human disobedience.

2. This disobedience cannot be a matter of irritation and accusation to those who have themselves come to obey the Gospel, to the Apostle and with him the whole Church, which consists of so many Gentiles and so remarkably few Jews. For this disobedience means to the disobedient exclusion from the benefit of the Gospel and therefore from all that God wills with man through the Gospel: exclusion from participating in his glorification in the world. The disobedient have consequently been hurt and punished by their disobedience. This is a double punishment because their disobedience consists in their failure – which is simply incomprehensible – as regards the very grace of God bestowed upon them. They ought not to be accused but pitied. Not as an Israelite patriot but as an Apostle he has this 'great sorrow and unceasing pain' on their

account, that is what Paul in 9.2 has to admit is his attitude in this matter.

3. According to 9.1 Paul has in the most solemn way made that pain the subject of his preaching. He is speaking 'the truth in Christ' on the matter, for what he now has to say he appeals to the testimony of the Holy Spirit. He regards it as worthwhile and necessary to keep the church in Rome with its Gentile majority – these believers, these obedient men – occupied for three full chapters with the problem of disobedience, the problem of Israel. What is more, he does this by appealing to them to share in his pain. But actually he says even more than that. In 9.3 he has the audacity to say that he could wish to be anathema from Christ for the sake of his disobedient brethren.

If this is not a rash exaggeration, it must mean that he, the one who has become obedient, Paul, the Apostle of Jesus Christ, can in no circumstances and in no way remain satisfied with the fact of Israel's disobedience and exclusion. Just because he is obedient, he depends on the disobedient not remaining disobedient. Were they to remain disobedient, he too would want to be, he too would be excluded from the Gospel, from its glory and from the service of God's praise. We repeat: this is no human loyalty speaking. The cause itself, the Gospel, demands the full unconditional solidarity of the obedient with the disobedient. For this is not Paul's private business. He preaches it to the Christians in Rome as the 'truth in Christ' which is as valid for them as it is for him.

And now there are three lines of thought in which Paul demonstrates his attitude, or rather the attitude which the Gospel demands of the Christian Church, towards the disobedience to the Gospel embodied in Israel. All three have in common the fact that they show that this disobedience in all its fearfulness is also in the light – really in the light – of the Gospel against which it is directed. None of the three say that there is a damnation corresponding to this disobedience. They say that both this disobedience and the damnation that corresponds to it are encompassed by God's way and work, by the way and work of his mercy – the same divine mercy in which those who are in Christ Jesus, who are obedient to the Gospel may glory even now. How can they do this, if they do not give and leave to God's mercy the first and the last word as far as the disobedient are concerned as well?

In 9.6-29 Paul declares that even the fearful event of disobedience betrays that it is encompassed by the divine work of mercy, because it shows that men when they become obedient to the Gospel do not choose what they deem good but choose the sovereign will of God. They *are* elect in their *becoming obedient*! We can therefore ultimately not be scandalized when we see many – the disobedient – who do not do this. In 9.30-10.21 Paul says that what they do in their disobedience is for this reason inexcusable, but that at the same time it is not without hope. The God against whom they sin is the very God who has decided and is prepared, with his righteousness, to take the responsibility for their iniquity. He has made faith in himself so self-evident to them too that it has been made objectively impossible for them to mistake it. And in 11.1-36 Paul says that God ever and again awakens obedience among the disobedient; on the other hand, as far as the disobedient are concerned, the obedient have only reason to show even more gratitude for the mercy bestowed on them by renewed obedience. In particular they ought to apply the promise from which they themselves live to the disobedient as well. This sums up Paul's application of the Gospel to the problem of disobedience to the Gospel.

The argument in 9.6-29 is governed by 9.6a: God's word, the Gospel, which was also, and originally even in the first place particularly given to Israel has not been annulled, superseded or checked on account of Israel's disobedience. In its way it is even confirmed by the existence of the disobedient.

The presupposition of the first line of thought, and this is according to 9.1-5, Paul's first concern is that disobedience means exclusion from God's beneficial work in the Gospel as well as from the active participation in the glorification of God allotted to man by the Gospel. But such exclusion belongs to the fulfilment of God's word, to the work of the Gospel. As we have certainly learned clearly enough from Chapters 1-8 such exclusion excludes man from God in every respect, i.e. it characterizes him in every respect as disobedient. Only then does it include and admit him as such, and allot to him God's gift and commandment. He has died in Jesus Christ and only in him he has been raised from the dead; this is the content of God's word to every man. When we see people who are excluded we ought not to regard them as excluded *from* the Gospel, but as excluded *by* the Gospel. When we see the Synagogue excluded on account of its unbelief, we must neither despair of the Gospel nor of the people gathered there in darkness. We must rather make it clear to ourselves that particularly at the place where it originated, particularly where it is at home, the Gospel has always brought about that exclusion: not for the sake of exclusion but for the sake of inclusion, but nevertheless there is this exclusion. 'They are not all Israel, which are of Israel. And they are not all children of Abraham, because they are descended from Abraham!' (9.6f). For what matters about Israel is not Israel, but the Christ promised to Israel, and Israel only for his sake. Israel must die with him in order to live with him. And God's sovereign will sees to both.

From the beginning all through Israel's history this was heralded by that exclusion, by the fact that God's choosing is always accompanied by a non-choosing, his accepting by a rejecting. It was not just any son of Abraham, it was not Ishmael but Isaac who became by God's promise the forefather of the Christ and therefore the bearer of the hope of all Israel (9.8-9). And again of Rebecca's twin sons it was not Esau, the elder, but Jacob, the younger (9.10-13).

Who excludes the one and includes the other? Not the good or bad will of the one or the other, but the word of God that kills and brings to life, the word of his hatred and of his love

(9.13), which from the beginning was Israel's hope and therefore Israel's judge. On both sides this word is sovereign. This
word is the personal word of God's free mercy. And therefore
it decides for itself where it desires to dwell and where it does
not desire to dwell, where it chooses and where it does not
choose to take its origin in history. That is why the double sign
of acceptance and rejection already exists in the history of the
patriarchs. It is the *same* word, and what happens in Israel is
the *confirmation* of the same word in both its aspects.

The question of 9.14 seems obvious. Does not this exclusion,
brought about by the Gospel itself, mean that God wrongs the
excluded whose good or bad will, according to 9.10-13, is not
taken into consideration at all? When Paul answers this question
with that scandalized 'Impossible!', it is noteworthy that he
does not say that God – by reason of his sovereignty – has the
right in every case and with every man to do exactly as he pleases,
for some reason only known to him. That is certainly the
answer given by the Church's later doctrine of predestination
to the question of the justice of the divine election. But Paul
replies in 9.15 by quoting what was said to Moses: 'I have
mercy on whom I have mercy and I have compassion on whom
I have compassion.'

That means that the justice of the divine election, which
might at first sight provoke questioning, consists in the fact that
it is the righteousness of the divine mercy. What God does –
and especially what he does to the sons of Abraham and then
again to the sons of Isaac by accepting and rejecting – is the
work of his mercy which has no other ground than this mercy.
A bare sovereignty would indeed not distinguish the electing
God from a tyrannical demon. But his mercy – and that is the
point in Israel's history – proves that he is a righteous God.
For mercy and its practice is God's right. That is also the
decisive factor in the statement made in 9.16. 9.11 said that
God's choosing will must take its course against all human
arbitrariness. And this, it is true, is now repeated: over against
God's will there is no right and no claim of human will and

action, of human decision and achievement. In all that they are and become, Isaac and Ishmael, Jacob and Esau can only be at the disposal of God's mercy. Where God is revealed and acts – as has happened in Israel right from the beginning – no man can get in before God, every man can only be prepared for his service. Neither those who are accepted nor those who are rejected have any claim. Neither have any claim because both in their way may serve God's good will. He wills them both in their own way. He chooses to avail himself of both – even of the hated Esau!

Still with the contemporary Synagogue in mind, which has been excluded by its disobedience, this is now illustrated by the example of the worst persecutor and enemy of Israel, the Pharaoh of the Exodus. The fact that this name is mentioned – as a parallel to the obstinate contemporary Synagogue this is simply shattering for the latter – shows that the excluded are the disobedient. Note that the sentence does not begin with 'on the other hand' but with 'for'. It must therefore not be understood as a contrast to the preceding but as its continuation and explanation. The existence of the Pharaoh, or rather the word spoken to him is just as much in accordance with the righteousness of God's mercy as God's decision concerning Moses. God also 'raised you up, that I might show in you my power and spread abroad my name in all the earth'. Therefore Pharaoh too serves the 'power of God' which in Rom. 1.16 is called the Gospel, in I Cor. 1.18 the cross of Christ and in I Cor. 1.24 Jesus Christ himself. Pharaoh serves the proclamation of the Name, i.e. the realization of God's own presence, which takes place in his revelation. Pharaoh's place by the side of Moses is legitimate. As much as Moses he takes part in the execution of the same merciful will of God. By his contrast to Moses and in this relationship to him he demonstrates that this will of God is really not tied to the decisions and actions of any man but that everything, even men's evil decisions, are subject to his will. God, by turning to Moses, wants to reveal his mercy as such, as the power to bring to life. Yet, by turning away from Pharaoh, by hardening him, by making him obstinate and by steeling his heart against himself, God also wants to show that it is *his* mercy which he owes to no one. So he shows by the example of Pharaoh that killing of man without which it would not be his mercy and therefore not real mercy (9.18). God now wills the disobedient Synagogue as he then willed the Pharaoh. Just as Pharaoh did, it must and will reveal itself as a work of divine mercy which in its way is not less than the obedient Church.

Would the Synagogue really be inclined to retort, as indicated in 9.19: 'Why then does God still find fault? Who does actually resist his will?' Is their disobedience obedience because it has to serve God's mercy? This question would be unanswerable or it would have to be answered in the affirmative if Paul had (in 9.15ff) appealed to God's formal liberty, to the right of God's power. But he did not do that. He spoke of the right of God's mercy, and that is why the position is as it is expressed in the counter-question in 9.20: 'O man, who are you to remonstrate with God?' For you are the man, Paul wants to say, who as the object of God's mercy, are not at all in the position – you have no voice and no word – to ask God whether he has reason to find fault with you. You are the man, who stands before that God who (8.32) has not spared his own Son but delivered him up for us all – for you as well. You are the man, with whom God does not find fault, for the reason that he has held his Son responsible for all the faults he could find with man. You are the man whom God only confronts with his own goodness. Certainly you cannot stop him if he wants to use you and your resistance, as he uses Pharaoh. But how can this possibly be used to excuse or even to justify your resistance? How can *you* do this before *this* God? The greatest absurdity of the question in 9.19 is that it desires to turn the shield with which God protects us into a shield for us to protect ourselves from God, from God's goodness. The parable of the potter which follows (9.20*b*-21) repeats and confirms the contents of 9.18. In Jesus Christ as the origin and end of all his ways God confronts man with nothing but his goodness. In these ways of his – as they have been realized and revealed in the history of Israel – he is free and has the right to make and to use vessels of honour and vessels of dishonour, i.e. to raise and to introduce witnesses to the fulfilment of his divine purpose and witnesses to human incapacity as regards this purpose. The potter of Jer. 18 to whom Paul is referring is not just any almighty god, who as such can do whatever he pleases. He is the God of Israel and as such, in his accepting and rejecting, in his dealing with both kinds of vessels, he does what is right because it serves the realization and revelation of his mercy. With this intention he does not act out of an indifferent neutrality. To him it is not the same whether he introduces witnesses to his light or to human darkness.

This God wills and raises these and the others in such entirely different ways, his anger is but for a moment but his favour is for a lifetime (Ps. 30.5). And therefore the work of his hands cannot say to him who formed it: why didst thou make me thus? Therefore God as the Potter has not only the power but also the right, in the execution of his will, to give his actions now one form, now the other. The fact that someone like Pharaoh is now only a witness to the impotence of all men, neither forces nor makes it legitimate for him to be and to remain one. It does not permit him to play off the divine negation under which he stands against the divine affirmation that is after all put before him by the existence of the positive witnesses of God's goodness – as was done, for instance, by Moses before Pharaoh, right to the end. For such a negative witness has to testify to human incapacity only for the sake of God's mercy. How else should he, as the 'vessel of dishonour' that he is, fulfil his destiny, but by praising the divine mercy, together with the 'vessels of honour', instead of accusing it and justifying himself.

That this interpretation is not only a possible one, but the only possible one of 9.19-21, is shown by Paul's explanation of the parable of the potter, which follows in 9.22-24ff. These verses should be translated and paraphrased as follows: 'But what, if (the right interpretation of that parable were this, that) God, willing to show his wrath and to reveal his power, has with much patience endured the vessels of his wrath, destined to destruction, for the sake of making known the riches of his glory to the vessels of his mercy which he has prepared for glory – and as such he has also called us, not only from the Jews, but also from the Gentiles.' Note that the sequence of 'mercy' and 'hardening' (9.18), of 'unto honour' and 'unto dishonour' (9.21*b*) has now been reversed, and that they have now been expressly connected with each other, so that it now becomes clear that there is only *one* way of God in which he wants *both* to fulfil his *one* purpose. According to 9.23 the end of God's one way is not that there are vessels of mercy, but that *God* wants to make known in them the riches of *his* glory. The vessels of mercy are needed for this revelation! And in the same way 9.22 does not say that there are vessels of wrath, that God has prepared them to be such and has therefore prepared them for destruction, and not even that he has done so to show his wrath. Paul says in 9.22 that God has endured these vessels of his wrath, prepared as such, with much patience. And this is what 9.22-23 say in their context: God endured the one kind in order to reveal the riches of his glory through the others.

His will certainly has the character of wrath too. How can he have mercy upon man without being angry with his perversity? How can we have mercy upon man without judging him? But by means of that very judgment, announced in all those vessels of wrath and executed at Golgotha, God wants to save man and will save him. The announcement of this saving judgment is the history of Israel – hence the long list of 'vessels of wrath prepared for destruction' in the course of that history. Israel would not be God's people, elected for the sake of his Christ, if there were not constantly within it this exclusion and consigning to destruction, if there had not over and over again been such 'vessels of wrath' in its midst, and if it were not eventually, according to the message of the prophets, to become one single vessel of wrath.

But for all that, we must not forget the aim of this divine judgment. When it is reached, under the disguise of the most terrible negation of which in his Son he will make himself the victim, God will not say 'no', but 'yes' to Israel and in Israel to all men. From the point of view of that aim, the final word about these 'vessels of wrath' too must be that God has endured them with great patience, that they too have received a place and a share in the design of God's merciful will and rule. For the sake of the One who was to come, whom God carried through the pains of the rejection he suffered, he endures all the rejected, he also endures Pharaoh. He endures them so that they may meet with him who was to come. In this sense God does not merely endure. He wills them, as surely as his patience is no mere sufferance but a form of his creative, powerful will. This is the justification of his patience with the disobedient. But beyond this aim of his patience with the disobedient is the revelation of the riches of his glory to the others, the 'vessels of honour' prepared for glory, which in 9.24 are expressly identified with the congregation of those who are obedient to the Gospel, gathered from Jews and Gentiles – the Church which proleptically was already gathered in all the elect of the Old Covenant. The One who has called the Church is none other than that Potter, the God of Israel, who creates the vessels of wrath only because he wants to create vessels of mercy, so that these will in fact be nothing else but vessels of mercy, and that only the glory of God be praised among them, and no man. In the existence of the Church, in particular, God therefore justifies the duality of his action; he justifies that he is also the God of the ungodly.

The meaning of 9.24 is that God's attitude to Israel is the same as it has always been. He has elected and called us, the Church of Jesus Christ, to obedience, just as he once called Isaac, Jacob, Moses: manifestly in his mercy and not in his wrath. But if we look carefully, how do we stand? Among us, who are now the object of God's mercy, are there only those who were predestined and qualified for this because they are Abraham's children, because they are Jews? Or has not the mystery of divine predestination and qualification rather been wonderfully revealed among us in particular, in such a manner that now Gentiles have become obedient together with us, have been made participators of God's mercy with us, have been destined to glory with us? Gentiles: these are men from the vast realm of sin, revolt and disobedience, from the sphere of the Moabites and Philistines, the Egyptians and the Assyrians, from the very sphere into which God had seemingly so cruelly and unjustly thrust back Ishmael, Esau and so many others in Israel, up to the unbelieving contemporary Synagogue. The existence of the Church in which Jews and Gentiles join each other in obedience shows that even that sphere outside is not closed to the mercy of God. And so the Church proves God's righteousness, she proves that which had always been God's intention in Israel, for when he chose the one and rejected the other, God really wanted to make known his mercy to the whole world. By means of this nation in its entirety, including the rejected through its eventual fulfilment of its destiny in the bringing forth of Jesus Christ. Through this nation to the whole world – and therefore obviously to this nation as well. In view of the believers from among the Gentiles, so miraculously gathered into the Church, Paul quotes in 9.25-26 Hosea's words on the people of God, the sons of the living God, who once were 'not his people; the beloved, who once was not beloved'.

To whom did these words originally apply? To the Israel of the kings of Samaria, which had been rejected by God and which had yet been granted such a promise. And because these words have now been fulfilled in the calling of the Gentiles to the Church of Jesus Christ, they obviously also speak with renewed force in their original sense; they also speak of the rejected, disobedient Israel. Now that he has fulfilled it super-abundantly among the rejected without, how could God's promise not also apply to the rejected within, to whom he had once addressed it? And in 9.27-29 Paul quotes two passages from Isaiah regarding the fact that according to v. 24, believing Jews have also been gathered into the Church. They speak of a miraculously saved 'remnant' of this Israel that had revolted against God and had become subject to his judgment. In the days of Isaiah it was only thanks to God's grace that there was such a remnant, that the fate of Sodom and Gomorrah did not become the fate of all Israel. But this mercy of God was active and therefore there was such a remnant! This is how we ought to interpret the fact that at present there are also some Jews gathered into the Church. It is due to God's mercy and not to their merit. Their existence within the Church preaches God's grace to the others, the believers from among the Gentiles. They have only been saved by God's grace; how should this not apply even more to the others, the Gentiles? Think of the fire from which these have been snatched away! By means of all Israel, through the rejected as well as through the elect – and therefore validly *for* both – the end and purpose of God's ways has become manifest in the Church of Jesus Christ as God's mercy. And in this way as the justice of all his ways with that whole nation! This manifest righteousness of God forbids us in any case to continue raising the defiant questions of 9.14, 18, 20 in defence of the phenomenon of disobedience to the Gospel.

In the second section, 9.30–10.21, the same phenomenon is now discussed from the point of view that it was in fact human insubordination to the grace of God revealed in Jesus Christ, that was already the secret of the whole history of Israel. We shall now discuss how terrible and how comforting that is. While God reveals himself as the Lord, who in mercy, for his own sake, of his own free goodness, takes care of man, it becomes evident what man is, and what human guilt, inability and unworthiness before God actually mean. That is what is so terrible and at the same time so comforting about the phenomenon of disobedience to the Gospel. Man's own willing and running (9.16) can only damn him. He can never praise himself for his salvation but only God, and he is in fact allowed to praise God. That is what the obedient must learn from the phenomenon of disobedience, that is what the Church must learn from seeing the refractory Synagogue continuing to reject Christ.

In 9.30 the question of 9.14 is evidently repeated and now answered correctly. We shall not doubt God's righteousness – after all that has been said we have no reason to do so – we shall hold on to that which has come to pass in the Church of Jesus Christ: there are Gentiles who have in fact understood and accepted God's righteousness, his merciful will, although their willing or running did not procure it for them. It just happened. It was a resurrection from the dead; they believed in it and it therefore happened to them. That is the obedience of the obedient. A contrast to this (9.21) is Israel's continued effort to fulfil the Law of righteousness – the order of life given to Israel as the people of the promise and the covenant – by means of its willing and running, by means of its resolutions and achievements. The result of this is that not only did it not accept and grasp God's righteousness but also that in practice it did not fulfil the Law, i.e. the order of life it had been given. It does not lack all that the Gentiles lacked. But according to 9.32*a* where Israel failed – and this is fundamental – is that it willed and ran to satisfy the Law by its own fulfilment of its works, and not in faith in the promise it had received. For this is the meaning of the Law, this is doing the work of all works: believing in what God wanted with Israel. Israel has failed to do this, it has violated the Law by its very effort to fulfil it. According to 9.32*b*-33 it has stumbled over the stone, it has broken on the rock on which it should stand, on the will of God's mercy, which had to become its undoing because Israel did not believe and therefore did not obey it. Israel was put to shame by the very salvation which God had prepared for it. That is what human willing and running as such produce even under the best conditions, provided by God himself, indeed, especially under these conditions. Its work is the pernicious work of unbelief. Only God's mercy accepted in faith can keep God and man together and so save man. So God's mercy is the only thing that confronts man: its accusation but also its hope, as surely as this mercy is the righteousness of man's Judge.

10.1 shows how far it is from Paul's mind to abandon Israel, disobedient in its unbelief. He repeats the declaration of 9.1-5: that also – and particularly – as an Apostle of the Church he is at the same time a prophet of Israel and wants to remain one; that he is preoccupied with that disobedient nation in all his desires and prayers. Paul would not do so unless he were convinced that in that way he is doing something that is according to the counsel and will of God himself (10.21). Note that Paul fully grants that the disobedient have a 'zeal for God', that therefore he does not regard or appraise their disobedience as a 'wrong direction of the will' or anything of that kind. He does not regard their zeal as empty and without object, but as zeal for the true God. He therefore sees the disobedient too as men who in their way have to confirm the promise given to them, i.e. God's covenant, which was fulfilled in Jesus Christ. But their zeal is disobedience since it does not acknowledge God's promise as such and does not deal with it accordingly. Their will is directed towards God; it rebels against this its own object, therefore it is (10.3) distorted and twisted, an ignorant will. For they do not acknowledge God's righteousness, as the righteousness of his mercy. They do not know God as the One who wills and acts for them. They are unwilling to accept God's action on their behalf.

Instead, they seek to 'establish their own righteousness', i.e. to prove and certify themselves as men who are worthy of the promise and therefore entitled to its fulfilment. But exactly that is their rebellion, their disobedience to God's righteousness. For the promise of the God of Abraham, Isaac and Jacob, given and known to them, is waiting for their faith. If faith is lacking, then the Law is broken in spite of all the zeal concerning its fulfilment – or rather, because of it. Those who have the promise do not believe and therefore they particularly make manifest what sin actually is. God's election and calling, the whole grace of God as directed towards Israel is needed for this to happen, for this genuine, real, proper disobedience to come about.

In 10.4-13 this is proved by showing Israel to be the nation to which Jesus Christ had been promised from the beginning, so that the order, the Law under which it lived could from the beginning only be the Law of faith ('the Law of the Spirit of life' of 8.2). Because it would not believe but tried to establish its own righteousness instead, it had to reject Jesus Christ. And because it rejected Jesus Christ it had to show that in its effort to establish its own righteousness it has missed the faith and so broken God's Law.

And so Israel in particular has to show that man is a rebel against God's righteousness and that he is therefore completely dependent on that righteousness and therefore on God's mercy. For it does not say in 10.4 that Christ is the 'end' (EVV) but that he is the 'aim', the contents, the substance, the sum total of the Law, its meaning and at the same time the way to its fulfilment. In agreement with Matt. 5.17 Paul has previously stated quite clearly in the Epistle to the Romans (3.31; 7.12) that he certainly does not regard the Law of the OT as antiquated and annulled by Christ but, on the contrary, as fulfilled. And in what now follows he will not say one word against the Law. He will not argue as though the Law had had its time, he will argue from and with the Law, whose contents and everlasting validity have only now been properly revealed by Jesus Christ, who from the very beginning has been its content and its strength. To believe in Jesus Christ means obedience to God's Law. And now Paul says conversely: to be under the Law, as in Israel's particular case, to obey the Law, as is expected from Israel particularly, means to believe in Jesus Christ as the One who is the whole Law, its meaning and fulfilment. And that is where Israel has failed; it has been put to shame by the very word of God which it had been given, by the corner-stone which had been laid in Zion (9.32f). That is why its lack of knowledge (10.2-3), its ignorance is sin, disobedience.

The man of whom Moses says (10.5) that he shall live by the fulfilment of the Law, the man who means and wills the Law is Christ; he will fulfil the Law by his death, and raised from the dead he will live. 10.6 is therefore not to be understood as a protest against the contents of 10.5 or as its refutation. For the 'righteousness of faith', which is there introduced speaking as a person, is again Christ: he who hears Moses properly hears the voice of Christ, and he who hears him cannot fail to hear the call to faith in him so as to receive in that faith the participation in his fulfilment of the Law and therefore also in his life, his death and his resurrection which are the work of divine mercy. All that we read in 10.6ff is one invitation, not to any disregard of the Law but to this participation in its fulfilment. Its Law, namely he who is the meaning and the fulfilment of the Law, the unmistakable voice of the righteousness of faith in the Law, will not allow Israel to bring by its own effort the fulfilment of the promise it had been given – its Messiah and its salvation – down from heaven or up from the underworld. Such heaven and hell-storming thought and action has been rejected and prohibited as sin by the Law. By such thought and action the real fulfilment of the promise made to Israel can only be misjudged and missed by Israel (this actually happened to Jesus Christ) engaged as it was in such thought and action. That voice speaks: Jesus Christ announces himself in Israel's Law and that is why there is only one demand for Israel to fulfil: it must do what follows from the fact that (10.8*a*), while Israel reads its own Law, the Law of Moses, the word is already nigh to it, already in its mouth, already in its heart.

Which word? That very 'word of faith' (10.8*b*), that very Gospel that we, the Apostles, and the whole Church now preach to the world and therefore also to Israel. And what follows and has to be done? We learn in 10.9 that the important thing is that the mouth should confess what the heart believes. What should the mouth confess and what does the heart believe? That which can be read in the Law. The one who speaks through the Law to those who read it, the one who is the content of the Christian baptismal confession of faith; his fulfilment of the Law, and his life as the life of the one whom God raised from the dead. All the commandments of the Law want to guide, help and assist its readers to fulfil this one demand. That is what the ten commandments and the whole law of sanctity and sacrifice want of them. On it depends all that it promises man as his salvation, as his liberation from shame on condition that he obeys it (10.10-11). Obedience is faith. Israel does not believe in the One who reveals himself in the Law, who in the Law puts the confession of himself into the reader's mouth and the faith in himself into his heart. Because it does not do this but even indignantly rejects it, it is disobedient to the Law, disobedient to its God, a sinful nation. When, today, the Synagogue hears from the mouth of the Church her baptismal confession of faith, it ought certainly not to appeal to the Law, which prohibits the worship and adoration of a creature as the Creator, of a man as the Lord of all. 'In this respect there is no distinction between Jew and Greek.'

What the Jews now hear from the mouth of so many Greeks, concerns them as well. Indeed, it concerns them first of all and should be their faith and confession in particular, if they were really obedient to the Law, given to them in particular. One Lord is really Lord of all, and the man Jesus is this Lord – as the executor of God's mercy and therefore of his righteousness, rich over all and unto all that call upon him.

And before him all are poor, all are dependent on his riches: the Gentiles no less than the Jews, the Jews no less than the Gentiles. The praise of the Creator by the creature, but also the salvation of the creature by its Creator most certainly consists in Jesus being worshipped as Lord. The Jew should not merely know this as well, because it is preached to him as well as to the Gentiles by the Christian confession of faith. He should be the first to know it. As a Jew he ought to know it of himself, as a matter of course. Without being repeated, the accusation against Jewish disobedience to the Gospel has thus been rendered more acute in 10.9-13. 'Whosoever believes on him shall not be put to shame' (10.11). 'Whosoever shall call upon the name of the Lord, shall be saved' (10.13). The Scripture says this in particular to the Jews, in particular to the Synagogue, in which it is read so diligently. And it consequently says that whosoever does not believe shall be put to shame, and that whosoever fails to call upon the name of the Lord, is lost.

But Paul does not yet come to this conclusion in so many words. In 10.14f he answers a question which, after 9.30, seems to have no point: can the obligation of the Jews to believe in and to confess Jesus Christ, which was said to be inevitable – and therefore the fact that there is no excuse for their disobedience – really be regarded as proved? 'How shall they call on him (confess him as the Lord), in whom they have not believed?' (10.14a). That those who read the books of Moses can come to this faith and so this confession too depends on their being able to hear him of whom Moses speaks: 'How shall they believe in him whom they have not heard?' (10.14b). And did they hear him, when they read the books of Moses? Was his voice really audible there? Was there explanation, interpretation and preaching? 'How shall they hear without a preacher?' (10.14c). Did the written word really become a spoken word, a message to them? So that they themselves have simply had to become listeners, genuine listeners and obedient because they were unable to evade what they had heard? If it is true that this is all the case with the Jews, so that, according to 10.4-13, they can be held responsible for their obligation to believe and confess, then this preaching, which has in fact come to them, must have taken place in the message, the mission and the authority of him who is the Lord of the Scriptures, and who as such wants to speak to them with binding authority through the Scriptures. 'And how shall they preach unless they are sent?' (10.15a). In 10.14-15a Paul is apparently merely *asking*. It sounds like an exculpation of the Jews of the Synagogue. Are they really obliged to believe and to confess, are they really inexcusably disobedient, since all those conditions have been fulfilled?

I

But in reality Paul has provided the answers with the questions. Yes, he contends, these conditions have been fulfilled and therefore the Jews do have that obligation and really are inexcusably disobedient. That this is what he means, is made clear in v. 15*b* by the quotation from Isa. 52: 'How beautiful are the feet of them that bring the Gospel as good news!' The Scriptures themselves, in this case the prophet Isaiah, do not merely prophesy the necessity of believing and confessing (vv. 11, 13). They proclaim the reality of authoritative preaching which explains the Scriptures, which proclaims them audibly and with binding authority. Simply as Jews, and therefore as a matter of course, the Jews ought to have known about this reality.

10.15*b* is therefore not a devotional decoration. On the contrary, this is the verse in which Paul makes his point. For in this indispensable link in the thought begun in 10.14 he speaks of the apostolate of the Church and therefore of his own office. In this last part of his argument Paul proves what he wants to say about the obligation of the Jews and their lack of excuse, by his own existence as one who represents the preaching which is based on his mission, instituted, commanded, brought to life, authorized and sanctioned by the risen Jesus Christ. He proves the fulfilment of this last part of the prophecy of the OT by existing and acting according to it. Personally, or rather as the bearer of his office, he is the affirmative answer to the question whether the Jews can believe and confess. They can do so, and therefore they ought to do so, as surely as they cannot deny that they see the fulfilment of the promise of the messengers who preach the Gospel as good news. There he is himself, a Jew as they are, the living fulfilment of that promise. Now they can no longer say that those conditions have not all been fulfilled.

Therefore the way is now clear to the thesis that, so to speak, expresses the sober fact round which these three chapters revolve: 'But they have not all believed the Gospel' (10.16*a*). In an inexcusable manner they have not obeyed the word of the Scriptures and therefore they have not obeyed God. This has become a terrible reality. They do not obey the Gospel;

they except themselves from the 'all' in 10.11, 13. The Gospel has come to them too, to them in particular, not only as written in the Scriptures but spoken and heard by them, not merely in words but in power, as proclamation, carried and proved by the mission of its preachers. The excuse that they were not able to believe and confess has been made vain. Their refusal to believe and to confess is therefore no accident, not inevitable. It is transgression of the Law, disobedience.

Paul however wants to make this statement too in such a way that the Jew of the Synagogue, starting from his own presuppositions, has to recognize that it is legitimate. Hence there is in 10.16b-17 the quotation from Isaiah and its explanation. For the final conclusion of 10.16a has already been drawn by the Scriptures themselves. It has been prophesied too that the messengers bringing the good news of the fulfilment of all the promises will meet with unbelief. It has happened before that the authorized and sanctioned bringer of the message concerning the Servant of the Lord who suffers for his brethren, could finally only turn to God who sent him, and ask him: Why hast thou sent me? 'Lord, who has believed our report?' It has happened before that a prophet, and not only the prophet but God himself was entirely alone against his people. 'Faith comes from the report (EVV: hearing), as surely as the report is made by the Gospel' (10.17).

That which the prophet, and now the Apostle preaches, derives its power from its content as do the words of Moses. This power is the power of its source and origin, the Servant of the Lord himself, and therefore it is the cause of faith which is inevitably active. Unbelief where the Gospel is concerned is therefore impossible; the attitude of the unbelieving hearers of its words is intrinsically impossible – a disobedience which does not merely resist the prophet and the Apostle but God himself. Only God can therefore speak the liberating word on the things which are done in that attitude. With his lament the prophet has already called on God's merciful intervention in the situation.

Who believes? From man's point of view the answer is,

'No one!' The man will believe whom God shall call and awaken out of the universal unbelief – no one otherwise and no one else. And it must also come to pass that the Apostle has to lament as once the prophet did, if the Scripture is to be fulfilled, if the apostolate really is to prove itself as the fulfilment of the prophecy.

The guilt of Jewry, manifest in the Synagogue combating the Church, is therefore in its way also part of the fulfilment of the prophecy, and thus, however terrible, it serves to confirm the election of all Israel. This nation, disobedient to the Gospel, is God's chosen people, destined to bring forth Jesus Christ who is Lord over all. 'But I say, did they not hear?' (10.18). This is no mere repetition, though the question seems to have been asked and answered already in vv. 14-15. But the answer in 10.18 shows that this time 'hearing' does not mean quite the same thing. The question here is whether in the last resort Jewish disobedience ought perhaps to be excused, because the living interpretation of the Law by the One of whom the Law speaks in practice has perhaps simply not reached them.

The answer, given in a quotation from Ps. 19, makes clear first of all that it is not only possible but unavoidable for the explanation of the idea of mission (10.15) to think not just of the apostolate of the Church in general but of Paul's apostolic office in particular. For the answer in 10.18 does not say that there is, as Gal. 2 expresses it, an 'apostolate of the circumcision', a 'mission to the Jews', committed to Peter and the other original apostles, by which the Gospel was brought home to the Jews so that they were very well able to hear it. By the passage from the Psalm about the sound gone out into all the earth Paul means that the Jews too must have heard what all have heard. Paul is therefore referring to his particular office as the Apostle of the Gentiles. In spite of the division of labour he looks upon this office as the proper link between the risen Christ and the world, in which he considers the preaching to the Jews to be included, because it is the inevitable and practically even the first effect of the establishment of that link. Here we ought also to bear in mind that to Paul all missionary work is only a human and more or less indirect announcement of the event that first of all happened objectively for all the world on the cross at Golgotha and which was first of all objectively made known to all the world by the resurrection of Jesus from the dead. Because of the sovereignty of Christ's word, mentioned in 10.17, the Apostle knows that it has already been made known to all the world, and tells the Jews quite pointedly that they have in fact also heard it, because, together with the rest of the world, they have been objectively confronted with it.

In 10.19-20 a second supplementary question is asked and answered. It does not occur in vv. 14-15, and it runs as follows: 'But I say, did Israel not understand?' We remember 10.2-3. What about their not knowing God's righteousness? What is said there is not annulled here. But we now hear that understanding they have not understood, in the same way as, according to 10.18, hearing they have not heard. The proof is that which has happened meanwhile to the preaching of the Gospel in the Gentile world. Note that Paul does not enter into any discussion about whether the Gospel is comprehensible. The answer of 10.19-20 rather assumes that the Gospel is not at all something that is comprehensible to man. But then this answer refers to an uncomprehending people that does not seek God, that does not ask after him, a people by whom God has allowed himself to be found by means of the sound of his word going throughout the world, and by whose existence he has therefore given Israel a reason for jealousy. Uncomprehending people understand! Those who do not seek God find him. That is what has happened in the calling and conversion of the Gentiles to the Church. Their faith, their existence within the Church is evidence that they have understood. Can the Jews then still maintain that they cannot understand? Have the Jews not been chosen to be the comprehending nation, seeking God and asking about him? If they do not do this, in their case it can certainly not be due to their inability. They could do it, but they will not and do not do it.

Observe how again the argument begins from the work of the Apostle, from the life of the messenger who has been sent out to the Gentile world by order of his Lord. But note also how the argument is put forth in the form of scriptural evidence and not in the seemingly obvious form of accounts of various kinds of Paul's missionary experiences. This is no whim of rabbinic legalism. It is done because, with all that he has said in this chapter, including the last argument, Paul does not wish to deny but to confirm the election and calling of all Israel, bearing in mind its disobedience: its election and calling by that God who is merciful to this disobedient nation. Because Paul wanted to keep this purpose of all his thoughts in mind, he did not dare even for one moment to let go the support of the Scriptures. The apparent rabbinism of this chapter is the very thing that gives it its particularly evangelical character, in spite of the terrible thesis which it expounds.

10.21 concludes the whole in this sense. In the last resort the salient fact for the Church is not the Jews' sinful failure to hear and understand – it is not the disobedience of the Jews. It is the way in which God has been acting towards the Jews 'all the day long' from the beginning: he stretched forth his hand to his people, he did not become weary of turning to them, of stooping down to them, of offering himself to them. Their guilt could not be defined more clearly and sharply, and nothing clearer and more comforting could be said about him whom their guilt concerns and who has made them the object of his mercy – who has not abandoned them for what they are, because his mercy is greater than their guilt and than all human guilt.

The third section, 11.1-36, is governed by the question in 11.1: 'Has God cast off his people?' and the categorical reply in 11.12: 'God has *not* cast off his people, his predestined people!' The question in 11.1 can be regarded as a continuation of the series of questions in 10.18, 19. Could the reason for refusal of the Jews to believe and to confess be that God has replied to the crucifixion of Jesus Christ by changing his mind about his people Israel, withdrawing the promise it had received, and turning exclusively to the Gentiles to whom the Jews themselves have delivered Jesus Christ? Are they perhaps disobedient because God no longer requires any obedience of them, because they no longer have any future with God at all? The question has certainly been answered quite decisively in 10.21, to the effect that there can be no question of this. But now in Chapter 11 this will have to be stated and argued directly and emphatically.

Paul begins his reply by first of all referring to his own case: 'I also am an Israelite, of the seed of Abraham, of the tribe of Benjamin' – like Jeremiah from the tribe which, according to Judg. 20-21, was once nearly destroyed, but then saved, and which was also the tribe of Saul, the king who was rejected by God. Paul, who as a persecutor of the Church had consciously and personally become an accessory after the event to the crucifixion of Christ; Paul, who had fully participated in the disobedience of Israel described in Chapter 10, he of all people had been called by the risen Christ himself and proved after all to have been elected: elected to be a holder of the apostolic office, to be the Apostle of the Gentiles. How could he admit that God might have cast off his people? Is he not the living evidence to the contrary, the evidence of the faithfulness of God's mercy towards his people? Is he not himself a fulfilment of the saying in Ps. 94.14: 'God will not cast off his people'? How could he of all people seriously fail to expect the fulfilment of this word also as far as the other disobedient men of this nation were concerned? Or should the existence of one man not be sufficient proof as regards the whole nation.

The answer is given in 11.2b-4 by a reference to Elijah, the prophet of the apostate northern Israel during its worst days (the days of Ahab and Jezebel) – to the lament with which that lonely man (like the prophet mentioned in 10.16) turned to God. But it also mentions the answer he received from God, which certainly admitted the truth of his lament and accusation, but which even so drew his attention to the seven thousand who had not conformed and who were not an irrelevant minority; who were, in God's sight, in contrast to the majority of the Israel of their days, all Israel, Israel as such: in the midst of the general rebellion kept by God for himself. Elijah was then not an exception to prove the rule: he was not the one swallow that does not make a summer, and neither is Paul!

In the same way there is now also a remnant set apart by the election of grace: 'But if it is by grace, it is no more of works, otherwise grace would be no more grace' (11.6). This is the application to the present of this word of God. Paul is thinking of the other apostles who, like himself, have come from Israel, of the three thousand of Pentecost in Jerusalem, and of the thousands who afterwards joined in their faith. He is thinking of all those from the synagogues in the other Mediterranean countries to whom he has not preached the Gospel in vain. The words in which Paul applies this emphasize that those seven thousand were not a praiseworthy little troop of the seven upright men; they were God's elect, whom God had kept for himself, and therefore they were the whole of Israel. Because all Israel as such was elected by God's free grace, and in order that the eternal destiny of Israel should be confirmed, such free election thus took place and takes place in time and within Israel. This election by grace causes the existence of the seven thousand righteous men, who have never been lacking in this nation, not even during its worst apostasy and under the heaviest of the divine judgments to which it was consequently exposed. In them and for their sake all Israel was permitted to continue as God's people in spite of everything. Their steadfastness and valour did not make them worthy of God's election; God's election made them worthy of steadfastly and courageously representing the elected Israel as a whole. When God keeps them for himself he therefore does not return favour for favour but deals with them as once he did with Abraham.

And this is the precious thing in which they, and the remnant – and, in view of the remnant all Israelites – may glory: the remnant as such is proof that God has not ceased to act towards

Israel as he has done from the beginning – on the basis of and according to his mercy and not according to human works – on the basis of his entirely free and therefore all-powerful grace. God ever and again acts towards Israel in this way, and therefore Jesus Christ, as the one for whom all Israel is predestined, is ever present and manifest to all Israel. Because that is how God deals with Israel. There is always – there was then and there is now – the Church from and in Israel too, and all Israel secretly lives – lived then and lives now – in her. The remnant of Israel, kept by the election of grace, however large or small it may be, is in God's sight all Israel. By testifying to this divine election by grace, both the story of Elijah and the story of Paul himself witness to God's constancy in the election of his people, and are a refutation of the antisemitic question of 11.1: did God cast off his people?

The question 'What then?' in 11.7 means: 'What is the meaning of that which has just been said and what are its consequences?' The answer is to begin with: 'That which Israel seeks it has not obtained, but the election has obtained it' (11.7a). According to 9.31 and 10.3 Israel seeks to obtain its own righteousness by fulfilment of the Law, and by its own achievements to fulfil its destination to be Israel, God's champion. But as was shown in Chapter 10 and need not be shown again, it did not achieve this but the reverse.

In 9.30 it said that the Gentiles have in fact obtained the righteousness they had not sought, and in 10.20 it said that God allows himself to be found by those who have not sought him; similarly it is now impossible that that which is said about Israel in 11.7a should be the final word. What Israel in general did not obtain has in fact been obtained, in ancient times and now by 'the election', i.e. by that remnant that has its foundation in God's election – that has in fact been obtained by God himself who chooses according to his grace. The seven thousand obtained righteousness before God, i.e. they obtained that state before God which corresponds and complies with Israel's destiny to be God's champion, because God sought and found them as he did the Gentiles. They show that God loved and has not ceased to love Israel and that the calling of the Gentiles must only be regarded as the revelation of the depth and the width of the calling of Israel. In those seven thousand Israel comes into its own: *nota bene*, Israel, in exactly the same way as the Gentiles, no differently from them. Israel comes into its own as the people to whom God became manifest though they had not inquired of him, as the people of the divine election by grace. Because to Paul everything depends on this – because this alone is the hope of all Israel – he now continues in sharp contrast: 'the rest were hardened' (11.7*b*).

After 11.11 and all that follows there this can certainly not mean that the others were abandoned by God. It certainly does mean that in and with the history of Israel which as such is a history of salvation, there always was and still is a history of disaster, a divine closing of men to God's promises and favours. God did not owe it to Israel that he should elect it, and he does not owe it to any Israelite that he should call and gather him into the seven thousand. Not a single Israelite has deserved this. By calling and gathering the seven thousand God shows his grace – and so the basis and the final certainty of the election of Israel, which also includes those who are not among the seven thousand, so that it is their hope as well. He shows it by the fact that there are countless people who do not belong to the seven thousand in whom he shows that his grace is free by not calling them to this particular testimony. That is the 'hardening' with which 11.7*b* is concerned.

The words of Isaiah, Moses and David, quoted in 11.8-10, are intended to make clear the way in which Paul understands and wants others to understand the first phrase of v. 8, 'according as it is written', and not in any other sense! In the light of the Scriptures, which in all their utterances are a prophecy of Christ, the thesis of the divine hardening can obviously not contradict the word of the Psalm quoted in 11.2. It must concur with it in proving that God has not cast off his people – and this to the benefit of the others in the nation, the hardened, the disqualified majority of the Israelites. For this is what those OT words say so emphatically: God, the God of Israel, is also dealing with those who are hardened – even though he does this by giving them a 'spirit of stupor' – and because he is this God he does not cease to deal with them too. God's table (the sum and substance of all his favours) remains in their midst – even if it causes their downfall as the rock of Zion in 9.33. We cannot find in 11.7-10 any statement that God, by dealing harshly with them, would cease to deal with them! All those OT texts certainly do say that God can and in fact does harden. But one has to read them in the context from which they are taken, to convince oneself: they all speak in such a way that not only the gravity, but also the limits, the end of this history of disaster become manifest. No attentive reader of the OT – and to such readers Paul addresses himself – could be in any doubt, particularly bearing in mind the OT texts mentioned here, that the last word concerning those whom God has hardened has not been said by saying that they are hardened.

This is now made absolutely plain by the question in 11.11*a*: 'Did they stumble that they might fall,' that God might drop them? and by the 'No!' with which Paul answers. When Paul said in 11.7 that the others were hardened, he said it 'according as it is written', as the Scripture says it. As he now explains, he wants on no account to be regarded as having said that God has cast off any of his people, if only those 'others'. What did and what does God want to do with them? By means of their stumbling (11.11*b*) salvation is to come to the Gentiles. Not the seven thousand elect but the very majority of the rejected in Israel, by delivering up Jesus Christ to the Gentiles for crucifixion, have opened the door to the Gentiles and restored the solidarity of sin but also of grace between Israel and the Gentile world. In the same way Paul himself was constantly led to the Gentiles as a result of his rejection by the Synagogue. The evil history of these disobedient people therefore belongs to the history of salvation in a way which is particularly decisive for the Gentiles. But what will happen to these disobedient people themselves? Paul answers that the very fact that salvation comes to the Gentiles shall provoke them to jealousy, i.e. from the mercy God shows to the ignorant and lost without, they shall learn who their own God is, and what he means to them in particular. Thus God, by hardening them, has eventually aimed at them particularly.

To understand them we must read the following verses in the order: 11.13, 14, 12, 15! The Christians in Rome know Paul as the Apostle of the Gentiles, and here in particular he asserts this, his particular office, with great emphasis. But especially as the Apostle of the Gentiles he cannot possibly disregard 'his flesh' (i.e. his relations according to the flesh, 9.3), the majority in Israel who resist the Gospel. It is the very glory of his office as the Apostle of the Gentiles to call his Jewish brethren to repentance. If he has to take the Gospel from the Jews to the Gentiles, then this can eventually only mean that he brings it to the Jews more than ever. The one whom he preaches as the Saviour of the world is as such after all none other than the Messiah of Israel. The mission to the Gentiles serves this revelation and therefore serves Israel (11.13-14).

Are then the Gentiles in the Church only a means to an end? No, not that either! For, conversely, the whole Church of Jesus Christ needs the Jews. She needs their failure: even this has turned into riches for the world; she needs their remaining afar off: even this has enriched the Gentiles (11.12); she needs their rejection: even this was the means of the world's redemption (11.15) – but she needs even more their full entrance into the faith in their Messiah (11.12), their addition to the Gentiles and Jews who already do believe in him (11.15). For when that happens will come to light what is as yet hidden even from the Church, then she will receive those greater riches, now only promised to her: then the dead shall rise (11.15), then it will become manifest and evident, that in the death and resurrection of Jesus Christ the end and the new beginning of all things have already taken place, that the Kingdom of God on a new earth and under a new heaven has already began in secret. What according to Ezek. 37 was promised to Israel will then be fulfilled for the Church, yea, for the whole world. In fact, what was promised to Israel – and therefore not without Israel itself, not without its 'entering in fulness' (11.12), not without the addition of those who are yet disobedient (11.15). The whole Church is therefore waiting for that time. Consequently it cannot object to having to be used to make the Jews 'jealous' in every way, she cannot object to her whole existence being one single act of mission to the Jews. Her own hope depends on the hope of all Israel. How can she then possibly think that God has hardened the majority of the Jews in order to cast them off (11.11)?

The second argument against this opinion is produced in 11.16-18: these Jews too belong to the original work and property of God of which the whole Church is the offspring, without which there would be no Gentiles in the Church, without which there would be no Church at all. 'If the root is holy, so are the branches' (11.16) – these branches too! 'When you want to boast, remember that you do not support the root but the root supports you!' (11.18). The root (the first fruits, 11.16) is the promise given to Abraham by whose offspring all the nations will be blessed, and the fulfilment of that promise which took place in Jesus Christ. As ancestors or relatives of this offspring of Abraham all Jews as such are branches of this root and therefore holy, set apart for the service of God as the root itself: all Jews, including the hardened, including the unbelieving Jews! Therefore the Gentile Christian must on no account boast of his belonging to the Church and compare himself favourably to any Israelite, even were he Judas Iscariot!

For in spite of everything the Jew as such, even Judas Iscariot, always shares in the holiness that can belong to no other nation: the holiness of the natural root from which Jesus Christ has sprung, and with him the Church. Admittedly there are (11.17) broken-off branches which no longer share in its life: they are the many hardened Israelites – and on the other hand there are live branches which once grew on a wild olive and have now been grafted upon the cultivated olive of Israel: an impossible parable of the truly incomprehensible phenomenon that instead of the disobedient Jews Gentiles have now entered into full possession of the salvation intended for Israel. Both are incomprehensible: the removal of the holy branches as well as the grafting of the unholy branches which are sanctified by this grafting. What advantage do the believing Gentiles have over the unbelieving Jews? Only this: that the holy root supports *them*. But it is and remains the root of Israel. How can the Gentile Christians have this advantage over the unbelieving Jews without recognizing in those unbelieving Jews too the holiness of the root which supports them, as David did not cease to recognize and to honour in Saul the elect and anointed of the Lord. He who has Jesus Christ in faith, cannot but want the Jews also. For otherwise he cannot have the Jew Jesus!

And so this second argument against any presumption of the obedient over the disobedient (11.19-22) quite naturally becomes a warning to the obedient, to the Gentiles in the Church who for the time being have been so wonderfully preferred to the Jews. What are you talking about? 'Those branches were broken off so that I might be grafted in' (11.19), that is the argument of the Christian anti-semite to the present day: the Jews have crucified Christ; therefore they are no longer God's people; and consequently we Christians have taken their place. 'Right!' Paul says in 11.20. Apparently he has said the same in 11.17. But this cannot possibly be meant in any anti-semitic sense. For to be grafted into live communion with that holy root is to believe, and to believe is to believe in the risen Jesus Christ in whom God *against* Israel has declared himself *for* Israel. The disobedient, the Jews have come to nothing because they do not believe. But even more would the obedient, the Christians, come to nothing if they were no longer to believe; if they were no longer to believe in the risen Jesus Christ. For in the resurrection of Jesus Christ God has made an end not only of the Jews' rejection of Jesus Christ but also of his own rejection of the Jews. He has once and for all done away with all Jewish pride, but at the same time with all pride, and therefore with all Christian pride. The man who believes fears God and submits to his decision (11.21). If the Gentiles were to be 'highminded in their thoughts' about the eternal Jew, they themselves would at once be subject to the same fate. They would then be in a worse condition than he in his because, in contrast to him, if they were not to believe and were cut off again they would lose everything. And there, in the resurrection of Jesus Christ (11.22), God has, together with his severity, at the same time revealed his kindness, and men from among the Gentiles have been permitted to see, acknowledge and believe it before the majority of the Jews. God's kindness is the kindness of the God of Israel!

What follows from this? What is therefore demanded of the Gentiles? That they abide by the kindness of God which is revealed to them. That is their faith. How can they in this faith and from this faith draw the conclusion that God must have cast off and dropped his people? They must have lost the faith. If that is their opinion they must themselves have been broken off again. Anti-semitism is a sin against the Holy Ghost, Paul in fact says in 11.19-22. The obedient must watch so that they do not become guilty of this most potent form of disobedience.

And now (11.23), while the parable of the olive tree and its branches continues to be applied and Christians are still warned, a new line of thought begins. For the first time Paul expresses in positive terms what has evidently been the aim of his statements all through this chapter: 'These too [those others in Israel, whom God has hardened] shall be grafted in again, if they do not continue in their unbelief. Just as God's goodness involves a qualification regarding the obedient, it is a promise regarding the disobedient: it has the power to open them just as it has closed them. Man's disobedience cannot confront God with an everlasting fact. God remains free as regards the disobedient, just as he remains free as regards the obedient. When

143

Paul remembers what has happened to those Gentiles who are now gathered into the Church, it is impossible for him to believe in the everlasting persistence of Jewish unbelief. Against the nature of both the wild *and* the cultivated olive (11.24) it has happened that Gentiles have been saved from their desperate estrangement from the true God and called to faith in him, the God of Israel. A creation has taken place. Grace has prevailed. As Paul is a witness of that major miracle, the minor miracle is to him a matter of course: Israel, which by nature belongs to the Church, will arrive there.

We must not forget that in the form of the Jew of the Synagogue Paul is thinking of the man who is truly sinful and lost. As far as that man is concerned Paul can regard the preceding as a matter of course only because of his faith in the all-powerful goodness of God made known in the resurrection of Jesus Christ. But in this faith it is to Paul a matter of course and he wants it to be a matter of course to the Church listening to him. According to the clear statement of 11.25 the 'mystery' to which that verse refers does not consist in the fact that one day the obvious will happen, but in the fact that it has not yet happened, that Paul and the Church with him still have to grapple with the riddle that disobedience to the Gospel exists too, and that the extreme disobedience of the Jews in particular is still a fact. Concerning this mystery, Christians ought not to regard themselves as wise, venturing the too obvious solution that disobedient Israel has been cast off by God. What they see, the hardening of a large part of Israel, has happened because the full number of the Gentiles elected in Jesus Christ and destined to become members of his body has to 'come in' *first*. They have to be called and accepted into the faith and into the Church *first*, *before* these Israelites, because the last shall be first and the first last. What they see is therefore no scandalous accident but God's order. 'And so (in this way) all Israel shall be saved' (11.26*a*), because thus and only thus this salvation can take place as an act of God's mercy by which the humble are raised and the high are humbled. This, says 11.27, quoting

Jer. 31, is his (God's) final decision concerning them (God's people), which is put into action in the forgiveness of sins. 'There shall come out of Zion a Deliverer, and he shall take away the ungodliness from Jacob' (11.25*b*). The last shall be first because the Deliverer will have compassion particularly with the lost. The first shall be last, because that which the Deliverer does marks those to whom he does it as lost. This is the way in which in Jesus Christ God deals with all Israel (gathered from Jews and Gentiles); that is why according to this order the Gentiles have to precede and the Jews have to follow. God's *mercy* must and shall be revealed to all Israel.

Therefore the mystery that confronts the Christian, the existence of the disobedient, the deadlock of the Synagogue is a divine mystery, worthy of veneration and not a scandalous one. The elect whose election is still hidden behind their rejection may live by the same divine mercy, which has here revealed the rejected to be God's elect. But their election stands (11.28) 'for the gifts and the calling of God are without repentance' and therefore irrevocable (11.29). In connection with this statement we remember 9.6: 'The word of God cannot come to naught.' God's word spoken to Israel partakes of God's changelessness. And therefore God's judgments and ways may be unsearchable and past tracing out (11.33), because God in his mercy has no counsellor by his side and no judge above him (11.34), because no one can live with him in a relationship of giving and taking (11.35), because all that takes place is of him and through him and unto him (11.36).

But what this praise of the divine sovereignty means, is unequivocally explained in 11.30-32. What is sovereign, unsearchable and past tracing out in God is his mercy, and man, whichever way he may turn, is eventually subjected to it. Faithlessness and untrustworthiness are not to be found in God and therefore not in his word, the reconciliation and revelation which has taken place in Jesus Christ. Those who confess to believe in this word, as the Christians do, must necessarily also trust in God's faithfulness towards his people Israel. The hope of those who base their hope on this word must necessarily be hope for the future of the people of Israel. Can God doubt himself? Or can the Church doubt his word? If she cannot do that, then she can also not doubt Israel's hope. That is why (11.28*b*) Christians have to regard the unbelieving Jews, those branches of the holy root – broken off but holy – as God's beloved. They must regard them as beloved by God because of this root, because of the election and calling which came to their fathers. This is the final word about them while the statement that they are enemies of the Gospel – according to 11.11-22 'for your sake' – hated by God, can only be of temporary significance; so that the Christians should commit neither themselves nor the Jews to it. Both the Church and the Synagogue, the obedient and the disobedient are dependent on the same consolation (11.30-32). Everywhere human disobedience is the beginning. The Gentile Christians do not owe their advantage to their obedience (11.30*a*). Behind them is, rather, horrible natural disobedience, unmitigated by any promise of law. They did not come to Zion, but the Saviour from Zion came to them (11.26), and that by the disobedience of the Jews, without which they would not be what they are. From what other point of view but this one can they then possibly regard both their own future *and* the future of the Jews? It is true that the Jews also have disobedience behind them (11.31) and they are still in the condition of the horribly unnatural disobedience of God's covenant people, who have broken the covenant. But what could be the consequence in the eyes of the Gentile Christians, but 'that they also find mercy', that they also participate in the salvation which through them came to the Gentiles. And in this case too an instrument will have to be used.

Reference is made once more not to the obedience of the Gentile Christians but to the mercy God has bestowed on them. The action of God's mercy towards the Jews has been inaugurated and set in motion by the fact that the Gentile Christians are there as people on whom God has had mercy. For the second half of 11.31 says '. . . that in consequence of the mercy shown to you they also may *now* obtain mercy.' That means that the Christians must not postpone to the last day this attitude to the Jewish question, but that now, today, they are responsible for the Jews' obtaining mercy through the mercy bestowed on them. In relation to Jesus Christ they are all together (11.32) included in disobedience, the Gentiles in natural, the Jews in unnatural disobedience: they have all been put by God into the prison they have deserved. And in Christ God has also destined them all to participate in his mercy and so to be free. That is the knowledge in which those who are now obedient ought to regard those who are now disobedient: in this knowledge they ought to think of their future. That is how the Gospel answers those who despise it, for that is how Jesus Christ answers those who have rejected him. Any other answer could only be an unevangelical, an unchristian one.

The Gospel among the Christians[1]

THE *Gospel in the Church* would be another suitable title for this last main section of the Epistle to the Romans, or, referring back to Chapters 9-11, *The Gospel and the obedient.*

'I exhort you' (EVV: 'I beseech you') Paul at once begins in 12.1. Note the difference: when he directs his attention to those who are disobedient to the Gospel, his appeal is concealed almost entirely in the glory and praise of God's work and way. But as soon as he looks back to the Church and thinks of the Christians as men who are obedient to the Gospel, the emphasis (we could already notice this in 11.16f) is on appealing to them and exhorting them. According to 8.28ff and all that was said in Chapters 9-11 obedience to the Gospel is entirely dependent on God's grace, which chooses freely. That is why those who obey the Gospel are in special need of exhortation. They obviously do not keep a stock of obedience: it must be rendered and accomplished from moment to moment. They may and must *live* by and with God's grace.

In view of this the Gospel, or rather, the immediate consequence of the Gospel, always is exhortation also, not addressed to the disobedient but to the obedient. To those who have obtained it by the Gospel grace in itself and as such is the inescapable exhortation: not to dispute God's grace but always and everywhere to abide by it as the power that dominates their lives. The whole Church exists by hearing this exhortation: By means of the hearing of this exhortation that which

[1] Cf. *KD*, II, 2, pp. 794f, 802f, 814f. (ET pp. 711f, 717ff, 728f.)

we call the Christian life comes into being, even in its details.

In Chapters 12-15 Paul writes to the Church in Rome telling them one or two things about the form of the Christian life. It is not a thing apart from obedience to the Gospel. It is simply the fact of man's performing it; it is simply man's continual confirmation and announcement that he believes, not just once but again and again, not with just one thought but with all his thoughts, not only with his mind but with his whole person, not only in some aspects of his existence but in all of them. In the Christian life it is continually made true that by God's grace *he, man* may believe and so be obedient to the Gospel. How can he believe as a Christian if he does not live as a Christian? The apostolic exhortation says that this is not possible. It tells the obedient man that by his obedience he has put himself into a position where he cannot do anything but be obedient again and again.

The Greek for 'to exhort' is richer than the translation conveys. It means 'to comfort' as well. By *exhorting* them, i.e. by strengthening them in the faith, by calling them to new faith, to a life in faith, Paul *comforts* the Christians in their lives in time and in the world. And by *comforting* them he *exhorts* them. 'By the mercies (literally 'the compassions') of God' – this addition points to the same interpretation: the exhortation does not appeal to man's reason, insight, goodness or freedom, it does not demand any kind of human return for the divine favour, but simply that they are the men on whom God's mercy has been bestowed. From this point of view they are exhorted and this is how Paul wants his exhortation to be heard and understood. We must note how the strong final note of Chapter 11 is resumed in this way (11.30ff): the Christian life as the life of the Christian faith is the life of those who from one moment to the other are kept by God's mercy and nothing else.

This *origin* of the exhortation leads immediately to the first summary of its *content*. By God's mercy, by which alone they live, Christians are exhorted to present their bodies – the whole person, without reservation of any of its elements or functions – as a living sacrifice, holy, acceptable to God. No matter who they are or what they are, they are exhorted to place no more but also no less than themselves at the disposal of the One who in his mercy regards them as worthy of belonging to him, whose good pleasure it is to claim them for himself and to accept them – their whole person – as a gift. The fact that it can happen that God takes a delight in these men, that he is prepared to have them as his own – this kindness of God – is the strength of the claim which is here made in his name. That is why the Christian's fulfilment of this requirement is called 'your reasonable (literally 'logical') worship'. It is logical, it simply stands to reason that the life of the man on whom God's mercy has been bestowed is as such a life which is intended to be presented to God. And the fulfilment of this purpose is nothing but your faith being lived – is the ordinary worship of you Christians.

This word of the reasonableness or logic of this worship also no doubt points in another direction: Christians are those who have been made partakers of God's mercy in the sacrificial death of Jesus Christ. Their life is consequently destined to be a testimony to his sacrificial death. Therefore it is itself destined to be a sacrifice of life to be presented to God. This sacrifice however cannot as such contribute or add anything to their reconciliation which has taken place in Jesus Christ, but it cannot fail to come about in endorsing imitation and grateful recognition of what has happened to them in Jesus Christ.

That explains 12.2: Christians, it is true, live in the world and in time, but by God's mercy it has been made impossible for them to adapt and to accommodate themselves to its form and character or to give their lives once more the form and character of this world. It has been made impossible for them because, thanks to their participation in the resurrection of Jesus Christ, they have already left this world behind them. Their share in the resurrection of Jesus Christ consists in a transformation which they have experienced. It consists in a renewal of their thinking which compels and also enables them, in the midst of the course of the world to which they too are subject, to distinguish between the law of the course of the world and the will of God, between that which is divinely and therefore truly good, agreeable and perfect and that which is the natural result of the process of the world. It compels and enables them, as men who have been sacrificed to God, and who belong to him, not to show in their lives a repetition of the pattern and character of this world but to erect a sign of God's will, a sign of the order of his coming new world. That is the way into which they have been placed by God's mercy, as men who for Jesus Christ's sake have been presented to God as a sacrifice. The exhortation, some points of which will be clarified in the following, is that they ought to walk in this way because they are allowed to do so.

In these last chapters there is on the whole no proper sequence of thought and therefore no particular arrangement. They differ from the first eleven chapters of the Epistle because the method of investigation and argument is here abandoned and instead we find something like a cross-section in which we can no longer recognize the principle of Paul's selection and sequence. Now and then (e.g. in 13.1-7, the paragraph on political power, or 14.1–15.13, the long final section on the strong and the weak in the faith) we may assume that Paul is referring to information which he had received from the Church in Rome, and which prompted him to these particular exhortations. The remainder was probably written with the Christian life of other churches in Greece and Asia Minor in mind.

We should therefore not expect to find anything like a systematic exposition, a kind of Christian ethics – not even in outline. While first 12.3-8; also 13.1-7; 13.8-10; 13.11-14 and the final part 14.1ff are separate units, complete and coherent in themselves, 12.9-21 is a series of exclamations which can only very artificially be subordinated to one governing thought. The same applies to all these chapters: they are practical, and they are confidently and visibly dominated by the fundamental exhortation in 12.1-2, but they are not a coherent whole, arranged according to a definite thought. As should be the case with genuine exhortations, these chapters speak of individual points and ought to be interpreted accordingly – always, of course, with that starting-point in 12.1-2 in mind, and in connection with the preaching of the Gospel on which they are based.

The exhortation addresses the Christian (12.3-8) in the first place as a member of the Christian Church. The will of God, which, according to 12.2, he ought to know and to which he ought to submit in distinction from the world, consists in this: that he shall regard and conduct his life in the Church as a service. That service is regulated by the fact that the *one grace* has been bestowed on the Church in the form of many *gifts*, which are not separate and competitive, but diverse, and in their very diversity coherent and harmonious. And the faith which apprehends grace as such and in its various gifts, shows (as *the* Christian faith) every man his purpose in common with that of all the others. At the same time (as *his* Christian faith) it shows every man his limitations. If the Church followed the pattern of this world, the thing would happen which is described in the warning of 12.3: everyone would rely on the power and the right of his own vitality, and stray without limitation. But, discharging the duties of his office, which he himself has received by grace, in order that he should preach grace as the authority and order valid in the Church, the Apostle tells every man to make fruitful the renewal of his mind which has come about by directing his attention to nothing but 'what is becoming' (acceptable, RV), by thinking 'so as to think soberly', which is immediately explained as 'starting and completing the course of his Christian faith which God has destined to him' (12.3; RV: 'according as God hath dealt to each man a measure of faith'). He so lives in the Church, in which every individual lives as a member of the body in the fulness of the whole, that he is faithful to his particular place and function, which he has not chosen and fixed, but which has been allotted to him (12.4-5).

God's grace itself is undivided, one and the same for all. But its gifts are many, not according to the diversity of human dispositions, temperaments and inclinations but according to the diversity of God's will to which we must all in our faith render obedience, if we do not wish to forfeit the divine mercy which alone holds us. This is in marked contrast to man's natural vitality without grace and without limits. Within these terms the exhortation – as the end, 12.6-8, shows – can say that everyone shall accomplish, live and effect the task he has been given and set by God's will, exactly as God has given and set it. And this very obedience ought also, in every respect, to be his freedom. Let the riches of the whole be also his own personal riches.

For here, as well as in I Cor. 12, the separate definition of the gifts of grace hinders from the beginning the threat of the abuse that this positive side of the exhortation might involve. It is not a question of individual dispositions, inclinations or desires, but of the prophetic word, the service of love, the work of teaching, exhortation, giving, ruling, deeds of compassion. With all this the Church, and therefore also the individuals in the Church do not serve themselves or the people in the Church or in the world, or even the Church as such; they have to serve God in the Church and therefore God in the world. They have to put his light on the lampstand that it may shine in the darkness. These are the gifts of grace. And because they are, the exhortation can only mean that we should take and use them. The wisdom which was referred to in the beginning, cannot be lost. In contrast to all worldly-wise caution it must and shall be fully honoured, where the important thing is really to accomplish, live and work *these* gifts, which are manifestly meant for *this* purpose (in the unity of the grace which they all represent). It would be rash for anyone not to do this!

We have now come to a series of loosely connected instructions (12.9-21) – in Greek 12.9-17 are an almost uninterrupted series of participle clauses – in which the life of the individual Christian as such is regarded from the point of view of this living together: first of all with other individuals within the Church and then also outside the Church. How does one live together with other people as a man sacrificed to God (12.1), in accordance with the renewal of our thinking that has happened, distinguishing God's will from the form of this world (12.2)? This is the question that is answered now. For a right understanding of each single word we ought therefore not to forget that they are applications of the fundamental exhortation. We shall only be able to refer to them briefly.

Christian love, as it is both permitted and demanded, in the first place *within* the Church, is 'without hypocrisy' and therefore sincere when it witnesses to our knowledge that God loved us first in the man Jesus. Loving those other people can and must be done both by abhorring that which is evil and by cleaving to that which is good, by a negation and by an affirmation, and in any case it must be done with discriminating wisdom (12.9).

But in the Church the common mandate, the service of the common cause is the important thing. Love must therefore come about in the intimacy, in the devotion in which we mean and seek neither ourselves nor the other, in which, in brotherly love, we mean and seek the common Lord; for this reason in this devotion we are pleased to prefer the other man in honour as a representative of that Lord (12.10). The zeal (EVV: 'diligence') must not slacken, the fire must not die, the service must not be discontinued, hope must not become joyless, our attitude in tribulation must not become inconstant, prayers must not cease, the needs of the saints (i.e. of those whose lives have been turned to the service of the Lord) must not be neglected (12.11-13). In this way, by doing all this, in this form of complete and incessant devotion, men love one another in the Church. Thus in living together with other people one is a sacrifice offered to God. That is the meaning and power of love when it is Christian love. It has the meaning and the power, the sincerity and the freedom, the infinity and the limits of supreme realism. It certainly cannot degenerate

into sentimentalism. And neither can it become tired or perverted into indifference, antipathy or separatism. It takes possession of all the emotions, and it has stamina, authority and
power. The thing that moves and supports it is not nature but
God's grace, the mandate of the Church and not individual
needs, the fear of God and not respect for men. Or, conversely,
it is nature taken prisoner by grace; personal needs which have
been accepted into the service of the Church; a respect for men
that has its basis and its limits in the fear of God. Later (13.8ff)
Paul was once more to return to this.

The Christian however does not only live within the Church,
but also outside in the world. In that very world to which he
can no longer conform! For the Church has been placed right
into this world: yea, she lives her apparently separate life for
the sake of this world! It is therefore all-important that – while
raising her protest against the form of the world – she lives her
life for and not against the world. Consequently it is all-
important that both the Church and every individual Christian
should meet the persecution which she suffers and which affects
every Christian personally, not with curses – as if one party
were opposing another – but with blessings (12.14). For this
is what Jesus Christ did to every Christian 'when we were still
enemies' (5.10). This has happened to the Christian, and it is
the thing to which, as a Christian, he has to bear witness, particularly to those who treat him as enemies. He certainly does
not go his own way. It would not be in keeping with the
renewal of his thinking, it would be too worldly a way of thinking and acting to desire to escape from the world. Stoic detach-
ment from the life with the people in the world has most
decidedly never been the kind of blessing demanded of a
Christian. He can only bless if he counters his persecution by
particularly living with the people in the world, rejoicing with
them, weeping with them, being human with them (12.15).

But even so – sharing joy and sorrow with them – he follows
a definite course, which is determined by the unity of the
Church and her mandate. He will not join in the particular

upward impulse and instinct, in the desire to be as God, which is so characteristic of the world which has not yet heard the Gospel. The Christian will always be found where God's grace in Jesus Christ has found him, in the humility of one who knows that, for time and eternity, he owes nothing to his own wisdom and strength in the lowliness of one – in whatever position he may be, in joy or in sorrow, in success or in failure, in the majority or in a minority – who has been accepted, whom God has admitted to his way and his work. A Christian can always be found where man's humanity is stressed in contrast to any likeness to God (12.16). If he does this he will certainly not render evil for evil, but in the sight of all men – whether they see it or not – he will stand up for the divine good. The divine good is always – and never in vain – with those whom God through his Spirit has made poor and utterly needy (12.17). In this genuine poverty before God the Christian will then be a living and straightforward offer of peace to all men: he will be the bearer of the divine offer of peace which has been made to them (12.18).

What if they do not accept this offer? And in spite of everything, they will not all accept it. Not all of them? How many, how few will accept it? Ought he after all to deal with them as with an opponent? Render like unto like, at least by dropping them now, ultimately and finally, as a picture of God's wrath, leaving them and going his own way? In 12.19-21 Paul makes it abundantly clear that for a Christian there can be no question of any retaliation but that of rendering good for evil, in other word the sharing mentioned in 12.15. He would himself have to give up the grace bestowed on him if he wanted to apply to other men God's wrath and vengeance of his grace. It is for God alone to witness to his wrath and vengeance – with the exception of the special commission that will be mentioned later.

It is the task of the Church and therefore of every individual Christian to render unlike for like, and thus to fight and defeat the enemy – the man who does not accept the offer of peace – by simply ignoring his enmity and to defy his enmity by not allowing it to have the effect of making him an enemy in turn. The Christian will win the day over his enemy, he will 'heap coals of fire upon his head' by treating him too as someone in need, hungry and thirsty; he will consequently give his enemy food and drink instead of assuming the task of an executor of God's judgment and making the one who is already poor poorer still. And he does all this – how thoroughly Nietzsche misunderstood the implications of the Gospel – not in weakness but in strength, not because of a feeling of inferiority but out of royal superiority, not yielding but offering real resistance, bearing the victory, proving that as a Christian he is not overcome by evil but in a position to overcome evil with good.

The following famous verses on the *authority of the state* (13.1-7) are no exception to this fundamental rule of the relationship of the Christian to the world. They make it clear that no one need be afraid or hope that universal chaos will break out as a result of the carrying out of this rule. Just as and because God has founded the Christian Church in the midst of the world as his offer of peace to all men, with the charge to overcome evil with good, and armed solely with the power and the right of her poverty, of her living in complete dependence on his mercy - he has also established, in the world itself, an order, by whose existence and administration care has been taken that God's wrath and vengeance too (12.19) are attested before all men, that beside the offer of peace conveyed to them by the Christian Church, evil and evil men are therefore shown their limits and cannot take their free course, even where the Gospel does not yet find obedience, or no longer finds it.

And on the other hand these verses say that Christians ought to adapt and adjust themselves to this order for the sake of their conscience and therefore voluntarily and of their own accord, so that 'reasonable service' (12.2) ought also to have the form of the political service of God (cf. 12.4, 5, 6).

The powers mentioned in 13.1ff are in fact what we call the State authorities. The translation 'higher authorities' ('*Obrig-*

keit') has caused much confusion because this has been regarded too exclusively as referring to the executive authorities and too little as applying to the active co-operation of those who are being governed – which, in one way or the other, is indispensable. The word is the same as that used in Matt. 28.18: '*All* authority has been given unto me in heaven and on earth' – the same word that is used in the NT to indicate a certain group of angelic powers. This is enough to show that Paul has no intention of speaking here about an authority based on the 'law of nature', independent of the authority of Jesus Christ. Not a word suggests that Paul in these verses suddenly ceases to exhort 'by the mercies of God' (12.1), that he no longer appeals to Christians as such and therefore to their obedience to Jesus Christ. Because Jesus Christ is the head of his body the Church, he is, according to Col. 1.16f also the One through whom and in view of whom all things were created: all 'thrones, dominions, principalities and powers'.

That also applies to the authority of the State. It does not belong to the Church, but it does belong to the realm of Christ. Consequently everyone – particularly everyone in the Church – has to adapt and adjust himself to the authority of the State (13.1). Adjustment is the word, not blind subjection: something which we can safely say is entirely unknown in the Bible. Wherever such authority of the State exists it has been ordained by God – of course not to the extent that it may be behaving as its opposite, as revolution, as anarchy – so that everyone wanting to throw it off, to resist it, would be resisting God's order (13.2). To those who do good, to the Christians, those who rule in the name and by mandate of the authority of the State cannot be objects of fear: they cannot be strangers to be kept at a distance. This they are to the wicked, to the very people to whom the Christians have so far apparently made their offer of peace in vain. Because there is the authority of the State they are restrained. They are warned by it not to go too far in their evil courses. The Christian, the man who does the good and who carries the message of the triumph of good, certainly need not be afraid of the State's authority and of those who represent it. He need not keep away from them: he will rather recognize in their function the performing of a service to God. He would only need to be afraid and to keep at a distance if he were to let go of the grace that holds him: if he were to conform to the world and so do evil himself (13.3-4).

The authority of the State is effective authority: it carries the sword – not in vain, not just for show. And where it is ordained by God it does not do this at random, but against wrongdoers. In itself it might therefore very well cause fear and stimulate thoughts of escape. It has to bear witness to neither more nor less than the judgment of God's wrath on the evildoer. And how should any man, including the Christian, not be afraid of that testimony? If he desired to do evil and did it – and what but God's grace prevents him – he too could only be afraid. He would fear the intimation of the eternal judgment in the form of the earthly judge (13.4). He is kept by God's grace, and he therefore can and must adapt himself without the fear out of which the others adapt and adjust themselves. He must do it 'for conscience sake', because of his knowledge of God and his Lordship, because he knows and desires that God is praised by the establishment and maintenance of this order too, that God in fact has his servants in the representatives of this order – no matter whether they believe or not – because outside the Church the realm of Christ and its sanctifying power has this form too (13.5). Adaptation and adjustment means 'actively doing what is necessary for the maintenance and the accomplishment of this order, by rendering tax, duty, respect and honour' (13.6-7). Adaptation and adjustment thus mean to show one's responsibility in practical decisions too. It means to be within and not outside here as well. Christians are here under the order of God – the order of the one God – just as they are in the Church. And in both places they are this completely, as people who have been sacrificed to God; in the former place in a different way from the latter, but in both completely: in the State as well as in the Church, because they are allowed, because they are kept and sustained by God's grace.

In the section 13.8-10 Paul returns emphatically to the thought and theme of 12.9-13. The passage in 13.8 is not as simple as it appears at first sight. It does not say 'owe no man anything except to love him'. It says 'owe no man anything save to love one another'. Paul thus says that all that Christians owe the world can be summed up in the commandment to love one another. This would be an unbearable saying if the concept of Christian love (12.9-13) had not already been explained in the following way: the love that Christians have for one another derives its basis and its strength from their common responsibility for the cause of the Church. This is the cause of their Lord and therefore significant and beneficial for the whole world. As far as the task of the Christian in the world is concerned, everything depends upon this common responsibility coming about and staying in being; his 'blessing', his rejoicing and mourning with other men, his standing up for the good in all circumstances, his participation in the power of the State. Everything depends on the Church being and remaining the Church in all these situations. This happens when this love is alive among Christians in all its depth, in all its radical, in all its hurting and healing, in all its dispassionate passion. In this love the Church is built up. With it the Church pays the debt she owes the world. With this love she fulfils every commandment of the Law, for in this love she follows the One who has fulfilled the Law once and for all. In this she confirms her faith, and so does every single Christian. If the Christian loves only in this high and objective way, then he will render to his neighbour, to every neighbour, what is his due. Then he will surely not do him any evil, but only good.

The section 13.11-14 is to a certain extent a repetition and explanation of the fundamental passage in 12.1-2. Christians as such must realize over and over again, and in every way that they can no longer conform to the form of the world. This is impossible, because the Christians 'know the season'. Every hour they grow more aware that they are standing at the turning-point of time and that they must act accordingly. 'The night is far spent and the day is at hand' (13.12). The turning-point of time has taken place: how can they fail to know this since they have believed? This change is continuing irresistibly. It is the sign under which all human history since the event at Golgotha has been placed, in such a manner that it must become more and more manifest. How can we fail to observe this, when today we believe again what we believed yesterday? How can we fail to observe this even better today than we did yesterday? And how can we observe it but actively? How but by rising from our sleep, taking off our night-clothes (described in 13.13) and dressing and equipping ourselves for the coming day – with the armour of light, with the Lord Jesus Christ himself? From the renewal of their thinking that has come about it necessarily follows that the Christians indeed observe the turn of the time, as it has already taken place and still is taking place. And that is the exhortation which the obedient in particular cannot hear often enough.

The section 14.1–15.13, concluding the Apostle's exhortation of the Christians and the practical teaching of the Epistle to the Romans, is clearly distinguished from the preceding Chapters 12-13. First, the extensive discussion of one definite question of conduct now takes the place of the many general and separate instructions that dominate the field earlier. But something else is even more relevant: Chapters 12 and 13 were concerned with obedience to the Gospel inasmuch as it was expected and demanded of the whole Church of every Christian as such without distinction. Without participation in the service of the Church, without living in the love on which the Church is based and in which it is constantly renewed, without being a blessing in the midst of a hostile world without the acceptance of political responsibility, without the increasing falling away of the ties of a human existence which in the death and resurrection of Jesus Christ has already been disqualified, no one could, no one would be a Christian. This is as certain as the fact that all these things follow from the renewal of the mind that comes about when the Gospel is received (12.2), when we put on the Lord Jesus Christ, as witnessed by our baptism (13.14). It is not merely that it can and ought to follow; it necessarily and actually does follow.

But according to Chapters 14 and 15 it does not necessarily or actually follow from this renewal of the mind or from baptism that the obedience of all Christians (the obedience of every Christian without which he could not and would not be a Christian) has the same human form in all and sundry. In 12.3-8 we have already learned about the diversity of gifts of the one grace. But there the object was the gift of grace, therefore the exhortation in 12.6ff could only be that everyone should make full use of the particular gift which he has been granted, according to its nature, and thus live the life of a member of the one holy body of Jesus Christ – that everyone in his own place and in his own way living that whole life and for this reason surely with discretion.

But the diversity to which Chapters 14 and 15 are referring has nothing to do with the diversity of gifts. The point here is much more the diverse *reception* of the one grace, the diversity, humanly qualified, in the form of the obedience demanded of all. There are 'weak in the faith' (14.1) who are contrasted with the 'strong' (15.1). Observe that Paul does not produce an argument or a justification for this diversity but that he is content to state that it is in fact there. Thus he does not say that this diversity represents a particular richness of the Church, that we could or even should rejoice at its presence as if it were a sign of life or something of the kind; Paul reckons with the fact that it is there and gives instructions on how to deal with it. It is not even as if Paul were neutral as far as this diversity is concerned, as if he regarded both possibilities as equally legitimate. On the contrary, he leaves no doubt that – not only following his own taste but as an Apostle of the Gospel – he regards one of these possibilities, i.e. that of the 'strong' as the better of the two. But because he assumes this he exhorts the

'strong' to the right kind of behaviour towards the 'weak', and
thus he obviously also reveals the other assumption: that some
'weak in the faith' in fact exist in the Church. He says that so
long as this diversity exists in the form and the obedience of the
Church, the whole Church ought to live, not in mutual recognition of equality, nor in mere mutual forbearance, but in
mutually caring for and supporting each other. This is not
because these two forms are equally good but because this
mutual care and support is the good that is better than either.
The only thing that deserves to be called 'good' in the Church
can in the last resort definitely only be the goodness of Jesus
Christ. He is the Lord of the living and the dead (14.19). He
has not served himself but he has borne the disgrace of those
who insult God and has thus served his neighbours (15.3).
While fulfilling the promise of Israel, he has also accepted the
Gentiles (15.7ff). That is the good in which the Law of the
whole Church consists. Bearing in mind this good the Church
has to find her attitude to the human diversity within the form
of Christian obedience and Christians must find their attitudes
to each other within these diversities. Submitting to this law
their obedience will be one and the same in this diversity.

There is a better form of Christian obedience. But it is only
humanly better; the point is not that the 'strong' have received
a better grace than the 'weak', it is that they have in fact received
it in a better way. For this reason there is a danger that they
especially might violate the Law which is over them as well as
over the weak, they that might sin against the grace from which
the whole Church lives. Their better might become the enemy
of the good – of the good which is in Jesus Christ himself. This
must not happen. The Law that applies to the whole Church,
the one grace that all need and which has been granted to all,
the good of Jesus Christ must also be triumphant in the *way in
which* they are its better recipients. If this does not happen,
then the strong are not only not better recipients of this good,
but they do not receive it at all. In other words even the better,
even the best form of human obedience to the Gospel is simply

measured, is again and again tested by whether or not it results in a real obedience to the *Gospel*? Is disobedience to the Gospel perhaps sometimes hidden and flaunted in the form of obedience of a better or of the best kind? Is this obedience in and in spite of its human goodness really prepared to let itself be judged and adjusted by the Gospel as its recognized law?

In the Church in Rome (as Paul had evidently heard at Corinth) this diversity in the human form of Christian obedience arose from a question which, according to I Cor. 8.1ff; 10.23ff also engaged the minds of the Church at Corinth. It is fundamentally the question from which this kind of diversity has always arisen. There were Christians who thought it necessary and right to lend a hand towards the liberation from the ties of that human existence which had been overcome and brought to an end by Jesus Christ, and which had been so emphatically demanded of all Christians in 13.11-14. They thought they ought to provide themselves with a mainstay and support for that 'casting off the works of darkness' (13.12) and, by means of certain measures chosen by themselves, ease for themselves the details of the great turning from the old to the new. They built a kind of railing which they thought would help them to walk more securely in the way which the Christians had been told to go. They adhered to certain principles by which they could always find their bearings on this way. They devised certain exercises by the help of which they intended to regulate their movements according to the word of God. According to 14.2, for example, they were vegetarians. According to 14.21 they also seem to have been abstainers from alcohol. And according to 14.5 they distinguished certain days from others by a different mode of behaviour. At other times, under different circumstances other measures have been proposed and put in practice for the same end. Paul assumes explicitly that they did this in faith, and consequently not in an attempt to fulfil God's Law by good works. To people who attempted the latter, and who thus aimed at a return to Judaism, Paul spoke in an entirely different way, as he had done in the Epistle to the

Galatians. The people referred to here do not desire to be saved and blessed by their own works. They wish to live by their faith alone, and they take these special measures to do precisely that, because they deem them necessary, because they do not credit themselves with the ability to win through without this support, these principles, these exercises. They are afraid that without this little self-help they may lapse from grace. Therefore Paul calls them – no insult is meant, he is just stating a fact – 'weak in faith' (14.1).

And he desires that the whole Church – but all the time he is addressing the 'strong' as representing her in particular – should 'receive' them. Receiving does not mean confirming their point of view, agreeing with them. But neither does it mean just 'putting up with them'. It simply means what it says. As people who in their way share in the common faith and want to be obedient (whether or not their behaviour is regarded as better or less good), they also, regardless of this peculiar way of theirs, ought to belong to the Church and be treated accordingly. 'Let there be no disruption in the Church because of their particular opinions'. It happens (14.2) that some in faith – not until 15.1 are they called the 'strong' – need not avail themselves of such measures: but the others, the 'weak', do. The first rule is (14.3) that the former must not despise the latter, i.e. they must not deny that their faith too is *deep*. And the 'weak' must not judge the 'strong', i.e. they must not deny that their faith is *sincere*. The man who walks in the way of faith (with or without support or railing) must be regarded and treated as one whom God has received. Christians are (14.4) servants who have to serve a common Lord, each one in his own faith, so that each one has in the common Lord his own Judge and also his own comforter. They cannot judge each other regarding the varied human forms of their obedience. To 'judge' is to exclude. They cannot exclude where God has already accepted, where God alone, according to his mercy, will decide on the loyalty or disloyalty of those he has accepted. Despising would be judging too

(14.13), as judging is always despising. Both are equally impossible.

The second rule is that it is (14.5) of the utmost importance to all that each one in his way – whether with or without support – is absolutely certain of his case, i.e. of the form of his Christian obedience. Each one must be certain that he really may and must go this way in the faith. Might not despising on the one hand and judging on the other both have their origin in the fact that the despisers and the judges are not fully certain of their case? If they are, why do they need to despise or judge?

But how is this certainty arrived at? A comprehensive answer is given in 14.6-9. Each one is on the right way – whether it is in itself the better way or the less good one – if whatever he does or leaves undone, he does or leaves undone 'for the Lord', for the sake of Jesus Christ, to affirm that he belongs to him and loves him, and therefore out of gratitude to God – for this must be the basis for this affirmation. Whatsoever is done out of this gratitude is as such a good work rooted in faith. It is not a 'work of darkness' (13.12), neither is it a work of the Law to evade and deny God's free grace – whether or not it consists in the application of that support, these principles and these exercises. Neither with the one nor with the other form of our obedience can he desire anything for ourselves. We can only desire to apply them 'for the Lord', to express our gratitude. For we can neither live nor die for ourselves. Living or dying we are the Lord's. By his life and death he has purchased us for his own, he has brought our life and death under his dominion and therefore into his service, he has determined that our existence, in any circumstances and in every way, shall consist in expressing this gratitude. Whatever our choice may be and whatever the divine or human judgment on that choice may turn out to be – what possibility is left to us but for every form which our obedience can take, every possibility of living our faith, to be at all events a way and an opportunity of manifesting this service and this expression of gratitude. If living or dying we are the Lord's, then surely the salient point also as regards the choice which we have to make between the forms and opportunities of our faith, must be that we must make this choice and abide by it one way or the other only as men who belong to the Lord and only to attest that we belong to him. If everyone does this – it is what everyone ought to do and trust and help his fellow-man to do – then each one can and will be certain, indeed perfectly certain, of his case. If you are perfectly certain of your case (14.10), why judge, why then despise your brother? How have you come to want to exclude anyone, when all your concern should be directed to not becoming weary, not doubting as regards the certainty of your faith, your service and your thanksgiving, when you ought only to hold on even more closely to that which has been commended and entrusted to you, so that you can approach your Judge as the One who has already promised his mercy and in his promise has already shown it to you, so that, finally, his judgment will ensure that you are and remain included? Does my fellow-man (14.11) have to bend his knee before me or do I have to bend mine before him? Must he praise me (my form of obedience) or I him (his)? Neither, obviously. We shall have to bow together, we shall have to praise the One whose subjects we both are, if we really are obedient to him in one way or the other – in the better form or in the form that is less good.

The third rule is therefore (14.12) that the responsibility which each one has to bear and to discharge each man must bear and discharge for himself, and just in this way in true fellowship with his neighbour. That is not yet the final word. What are we responsible for? Each one for himself, for his own services and thanksgiving, we were told. But in what do they consist, when their human form can be so diverse.

They consist in the fourth rule: that in following the choice which we have made, we do not give offence to our brother, to the other man, who believes with us in his way; that we do not tempt him, but that, as 14.19 says, we seek after that which serves peace and mutual edification. 'Giving offence' is not merely 'surprising', 'irritating', 'scandalizing', 'hurting'. The existence of the strong is very surprising and perhaps very vexing to the weak, and vice versa. That is what in fact usually produces this despising and judging. We are certainly not required never to give each other any occasion for offence at all. This could not possibly be required, for if it were, these diverse ways of living in the faith, these diverse forms of human obedience would not exist. That is obviously not what Paul intends to say – even if he does regard one as superior to the other. We are required not to judge, not to exclude each other. And this would happen if we were to 'cause each other offence and temptation', i.e. if we were to make each other doubt that each man can certainly only go the way of his faith, and no other way. The weak might tempt the strong to regard as indispensable something that is not indispensable to them at all. Conversely the strong – and this interests Paul almost exclusively – could become a temptation to the weak, to let go of their supports, their principles and their exercises when in accordance with their faith – if it is to consist in genuine service and thanksgiving – they ought not to let go of them at all.

In 14.14a Paul states quite firmly what he thinks of these measures of the weak: 'I know and am persuaded in the Lord Jesus that nothing is unclean in itself.' 'All things indeed are clean' (14.20). In other words, there is no objective need for these measures of protection and safety. They ought not to be regarded or promulgated as God's Law. The man who avails himself of them does so on his own responsibility. But according to 14.14b there is a subjective need for such measures; when by doing something that is in itself clean a Christian does something which to him, personally, is not the service of the Lord, nor thanksgiving to God. If he *cannot* do it in faith, then it is, to him, unclean; it is sin (14.23). It is this that the other, the 'strong' man, has to bear in mind. By his actions he must on no account cause the 'weak' man to do anything that to him would be sin. With all due honour to the objective cleanness of all things – with all due honour to his own cleanness in the use of all things – the 'strong man' has to honour, not the precon-

168

ceived ideas, the prejudices or the fanaticism of the 'weak' man, but certainly the 'weak' man himself, i.e. his faith. The strong man must bear in mind and consider the threatened purity of the weak. He must not cause him to do anything he might consider unclean; which would not be according to his faith. The position in which this might place the weak man is called in 14.15 'grievance'. Paul means the sad position of someone who has lost his only possible support. This can happen, indeed it happens inevitably if he is not resolute in arranging his way and walking in it, as he should according to *his* faith in God's word, as the particular recipient of grace that he is. If I am the cause of this it means that I am the cause of his disobedience, however right I may be objectively. And as far as I am concerned it would mean that I do not live by love, that I lack the element in which the Church lives. It would mean that for my part I fail to give the world (13.8) what I ought on no account to fail to give it, as a Christian. It means that I am destroying the Church I ought to be building to be a light for the world, and I am bringing destruction on someone for whom Christ died. Ceasing to live according to his faith destroys the weak man – even though there is a life in the faith that is objectively better than his, and even though I am very well able to give an example of this by my own life. If it is not and cannot be his life, I am tempting him and damaging the Church if I attempt to force upon him the thing I consider better. Together with him I have (14.16) to guard a 'good', to protect it from profanation. This good, the good of the realm of God, towards whose revelation the Christians are moving, does not consist (14.17) in the diverse human forms of our obedience as such, and therefore certainly not in the vegetarianism or the abstinence of the weak, and equally certainly not in my un-impeded eating or drinking. It exists beyond those contrasts, in the righteousness, peace and joy which are the gifts of the Holy Spirit, by and with which everyone may live in his way, inasmuch as it is the way of his faith and inasmuch as he remains faithful to it. We can (14.18-19) only serve Christ, we

169

can only please God and we can only be useful amongst men by constantly causing and strengthening each other to seek that particular way, and then also to go along it, whether it is ours as well or not. This is peace and mutual building up within the Church, and the achievement of this is the positive import of Paul's fourth and most essential rule. But according to 14.20-21 the application of this rule can even mean, for the strong man, that he in his turn will refrain from anything which would ruin the weak man, if he were to deny his own faith and imitate the strong man out of fear of him. The strong man would do this not for the sake of his own faith but for the faith of the weak man, not in order to deny his faith, not because he fears the criticism of the weak (like Peter in Antioch, Gal. 2.11ff), but in the fear of God, for fear of ruining the weak. The advantage which the strong have over the weak is that in this way they can help them: the man who can walk without support can obviously also walk with it; the man who needs no principles can obviously nevertheless abide by them; the man who is not dependent on exercises can obviously join in them at times. How could he be the stronger if he could not do that which the weaker man is able to do? And he will certainly do that which he can do *as well*, if it is a matter of not forsaking his brother, of not destroying the work of God which has to be done in the Church through his brother. If his own person only were at stake, his own faith (14.22a) would allow or even command him to go on his way without any support, without any principles at all and without any particular practices. But here this very faith can and will allow and command him to consider others, because he has this faith not only for himself but before God.

The fact remains that as far as the strong man is concerned there would be no reason for condemning himself, if he were to do that from which he is now abstaining for the sake of his brother (14.22b). He also knows (14.23) that he would have been condemned already, if he did it doubtingly and not in faith, not in full responsibility, not in the execution of the service and thanksgiving which belong to his faith, but merely because of an incidental desire. He knows that whatsoever is not of faith, is sin. And if he sees the weak man in this danger, he will help him in the application of those measures by submitting to them, though he does not need them; he will rather do this than give him cause to take a liberty, which to him, to the weak man, would be no liberty, because he happens to be weak.

We could without too much difficulty imagine a similar apostolic address and exhortation to the weak. But it is probably because the Apostle's exhortation is addressed to the obedient and not to the disobedient, that in this setting it is addressed to the strong and not to the weak. The latter could only be given confirmation and explanation that they are in fact the weak. They could only be exhorted not suddenly to pretend that they are the strong, the authentic and the better Christians, as is so often done. There can certainly be no justification for this. But Paul has refrained from reminding them of it in any way but by calling them the 'weak' and exhorting them not to judge.

All Paul's attention, the whole weight of his exhortation, is directed towards the strong. To them he admits that he is one of them and emphatically points out that, since they are strong they ought, they are obliged, to bear the infirmities of the weak (the others) rather than please themselves. They are the strong inasmuch as a life without supports or principles or particular practices is certainly more in accordance with the intrinsic character of their faith as a relationship to Jesus Christ alone, than a life lived with the assistance of all kinds of self-chosen human possibilities, commandments or prohibitions. But this better life must not become the enemy of the good (15.2; cf. 14.16). Any man strong in the faith who desires to please himself has a feeble kind of strength. The Christian does not live and die for himself but for the Lord (14.7). That means in concrete terms that he lives to please his neighbour – not as his neighbour pleases but so that what has to be done to please him is in fact done to please him. The Christian lives for the good which he has to guard together with his neighbour, in expectation of the revelation of the Kingdom of God; he lives for the edification of the Church. This cannot be otherwise, for the faith is a relationship to Jesus Christ alone (15.3). Christ did not live to please himself. If he had done that he would (Phil. 2.6ff) have regarded his divine form as a prize and kept it to himself. In fact he emptied himself of it, took the form of a servant and became like unto men: he took upon himself and bore the disgrace of those who insult God. The important thing about faith is that it corresponds with this deed of his, the more because in faith consists our only relationship to Jesus Christ.

How could there be a strong faith, how could there be any faith, if this correspondence did not exist? All the Holy Scriptures of Moses and the Prophets witness to Christ as the One who has humbled himself for us as only the living God can humble himself in his almighty mercy. Therefore, and only in this way, they attest to believers the hope, the perseverance, the comfort by which they may live, and beside which they need nothing for a life that is right in God's sight – a life which is fully sufficient for them, so that objectively they need not help themselves nor be assisted by others. Since the Scriptures witness to this Christ and therefore to this God (15.5-6), it is inevitable that among those who believe in him and live by him God restores the unity corresponding to the will of Jesus Christ and to his image, which therefore resembles neither the image of the weak nor that of the strong. In this unity both together, instead of living according to their own pleasure, may and shall praise God in the Church, and, as the Church, in the world. In this unity of the faith and its fulfilment in the praise of God they will accept each other (15.7), just as they themselves have been accepted, and have no existence as Christians at all apart from that acceptance. But in that acceptance they will have everything.

In comparison with this, what does their own act of accepting, their own better or less good way of obedience, mean? Again and again they must (15.8-12) simply think of Jesus Christ himself, who as the Messiah of the Jews and therefore as the

Saviour of the world has revealed and realized God's mercy upon earth, in order to make the one nation and the many together into one. That is the great acceptance and because of it there is a church of Jesus Christ in Rome too. What would the strong in the faith there be without that great acceptance and assumption of the Gentiles into the one people of God? And what after all is their contrast with the weak as compared to the contrast between light and darkness, which Jesus Christ has overcome? We notice that here (15.13, as already in 15.5-6) the exhortation changes into prayer, intercessory prayer in 15.13, in such a way that the particular subject of these chapters is mentioned no more. The only thing that is needed is for this prayer to be spoken and heard, and then everything to which Paul here (and from 12.1 onward) has 'exhorted', shall be done. 'Now the God of hope fill you with all joy and peace in believing, that you may be rich in hope, in the power of the Holy Ghost!'

The Apostle and the Church

IF we have perchance forgotten that the Epistle to the Romans is a real letter, written at a certain time and under certain circumstances by a certain man to certain other people, the final part certainly reminds us of it. For a correct understanding of the whole it is necessary to bear this in mind. The Gospel, whose contents and whose encounter with the obedience and disobedience of men Paul has described in this Epistle ought never to be presented and understood as a 'truth' existing in some way in a vacuum. According to the biblical meaning of the word 'truth' the Gospel can only be presented and understood as a proclamation of God's mystery taking place between man and man, and therefore as an historical event. For the One whom the Gospel calls God has become man. That which the Gospel calls eternity has fulfilled the time. That which the Gospel calls the Spirit dwells in mortal bodies (8.11). Never and nowhere does the Gospel exist by itself. It always exists at certain times with their peculiar circumstances: always in the definite persons of the messengers who bring the message and in the definite persons of those who receive it. And in the Epistle to the Romans it does not exist in any other way. The thing that makes this final part so important – in which we admittedly receive no further instruction on the main theme – is that we are made to realize once more that we are dealing with a letter, written in about A.D. 58 from Corinth to Rome, that we are dealing with the Apostle Paul at a particular stage of his life and with a particular Christian Church of the first period.

The first thing we read in 15.14-21 is written with reference to the whole Epistle. According to 15.15 (cf. also 15.18) Paul realizes that he has written 'in part rather boldly' to the Christians in Rome, that in writing this letter he has approached them rather audaciously. We do not really know what in particular Paul has in mind here: certainly not the prolixity of his expositions and certainly not merely the exhortations of the previous chapter, although the urgent tone he uses there when speaking to a church which he has not founded, and which he in any case only partly knows, may be one aspect of the 'boldness' he mentions. But if we give full weight to the impression which even now the whole of this Epistle still makes on people, it seems most likely that we ought to think above all of the exposition as a whole. Again and again we too have had to learn from its few pages much that was unusual and therefore amazing. We have had to follow the author along many strange paths, sometimes unexpectedly rapidly and at other times unexpectedly slowly. We have met with many radical and exciting statements which were apparently or really even dangerous and offensive in their consequences. What a lack of consideration for all other known Christian and non-Christian points of view and ways of looking at things! What demands were made on our ability and willingness to leave all the citadels and tents of freedom and slavery, of *bourgeois* and bohemian ways of life, of morality and amorality, of godliness and worldliness – and to keep up with the way of knowledge and confession which has been put forward here, always to follow round new corners!

Which interpreter would here not feel the urge to excuse himself by explaining that all this is not of his own making but has really come from the text? That fact, which we cannot fail to notice even today, was already noticed in the NT period. The text in II Peter 3.15-16, to which we referred in the first chapters, may now perhaps be quoted in full: 'Count the forbearance of our Lord as salvation. So also our beloved brother Paul wrote to you according to the wisdom given him, speaking of this as he does in all his letters. There are some things in them hard to understand, which the ignorant and unstable twist to their own destruction – as they do the other Scriptures. These words are apologetically but clearly referring to Paul's 'boldness' (and undoubtedly not in the last, but in the first place particularly the boldness of the Epistle to the Romans.

As our text shows, Paul was not unaware of the existence of this fact. And what does he have to say about it? Here we must first of all take into account 15.14, where he gives his readers the assurance, certainly amazing after everything that has gone before, that he is not only convinced of the abundance of their good intentions, but also that they are full of knowledge and able to admonish one another. What then is the purpose of the Epistle to the Romans in all its boldness? 15.14 says that it is certainly not to tell its readers anything new, anything else, anything different from what they have already heard and already know as Christians. The old message in a new way, yes, but nothing new! The same thing in a different way, but nothing different. A greater contrast could not be imagined than that between an apostle and a genius founding a new religion or school of thought.

In the Epistle to the Romans Paul has spoken as a witness to the risen Jesus Christ and therefore as an interpreter of Moses, the prophets and the Psalms. Consequently he has not said anything which in principle might not have been said equally well by any other Christian to anybody else. He has only repeated things which the Christians gathered in the Church have all heard long ago. He has drawn from the source of knowledge which is open and accessible to the church in Rome as well. He has stated and explained nothing but their own confession. If he has written 'in part rather boldly' (15.15) he has only done so to 'give you a reminder', and so to repeat what they already know, to put it new and fresh before their eyes. When he does this, that 'boldness' comes about. This simple repetition inevitably has the character of a revolution.

But why is this so especially when Paul does the repeating?

Why, throughout the history of the Church, has there always been unrest whenever Paul, and particularly the Epistle to the Romans, has been read attentively and interpreted without fear? When Paul says that he has given his readers this reminder 'because of the grace which God has bestowed on me', he is evidently defending himself against the suspicion that the 'boldness' of this reminder might be the effect of some personal characteristic, his Christian originality or some such thing. But according to 15.16 it is an entirely different matter: Paul has to write and speak as he does because his office is such an extra-ordinary one. What does Paul do? He preaches the Gospel. This as such has nothing to do with the work of a speaker or writer – even if it cannot be done without much speaking and writing. Actually it is the work of an assistant at a sacrifice, a Levite who has to prepare the sacrifice for the officiating priest. The priest is Jesus Christ. The Gentiles are the sacrifice. And all that Paul does with his speaking and writing is nothing but the preparation by which the sacrifice is made ready for this priest, by which it is made acceptable to God. It is a matter of the sanctification of the Gentiles by the Holy Spirit. And Paul's participation in this miraculous work of divine election and calling, when the barrier between Israel and the Gentiles is mysteriously lifted, renders that boldness to his speaking and writing, and also to the Epistle to the Romans. This office is his boast, his honour and his justification before God – not because of his human worthiness of it, but because it has been given to him by Jesus Christ as an auxiliary office in his own service. His office is the reason for all that may strike his hearers and readers as bold, as new and strange. Whatever he may dare to say and to write (15.18-19) – he will definitely not say any-thing but what Jesus Christ has made real by his office. He will witness to Christ as the Priest who is about to offer the lost world of the Gentiles to God as an acceptable sacrifice.

Paul himself is the first to stand amazed and perplexed before the fact of the miracle that now the Gentiles are called to obedi-ence through God's words and works, through the power of

God-given signs and miracles, through the power of the Spirit. Paul is confronted with the fact that he has 'completed (EVV: fully preached) the Gospel of Christ from Jerusalem right round to Illyricum'. The two place names in that expression ought not to be taken literally, but simply as indications of the limits of the area through which Paul had so far travelled. And of course 'completing' has nothing to do with the ambiguous modern idea of 'thorough evangelizing'; it means that all these regions and the people who live there have been reached by his preaching, that the light of the Gospel has been lit in a sufficient number of places to break the darkness which formerly completely predominated. In fact – without reference to the actual number of those who believed there and then – it is true to say that the whole area, that the population of the whole area has heard the name of Jesus Christ. And the principle to which (according to 15.20-21) Paul remained faithful during all this time was to refrain from linking up with any previous missionary work done by others, from 'building upon another man's foundation', and to limit himself to those places and regions where Christ was not yet known, thus learning the literal truth of Isa. 52.15: 'They who had not learned about him shall see him, and they who have not heard shall understand.'

We must remember the tones of complete amazement and wonder in which Paul had already, particularly in Chapters 9-11, spoken of this bursting forth of the Gospel out of the narrowness of Israel into the vast space of the Gentile world, out of its natural soil into this entirely foreign soil. This is not at all a matter of course: it is God's miraculous work and cannot be explained apart from the resurrection of Jesus Christ. This is the history that Paul had behind him when he was writing the Epistle to the Romans. He did not make this history, but he was active in it; he writes so boldly because he is a witness to it. He speaks and writes as though God's mercy has become a reality to him which is more and more incomprehensible, yet more and more tangible because he has been allowed to perform this service. Those who do not see God's mercy in this way may be permitted, may be able to speak and write less boldly and confront their hearers and readers with fewer questions and riddles. Those who are less amazed at God's mercy, at the gathering of the Gentiles into Israel, may in their exposition of the Gospel express themselves in a less amazing manner than Paul has done; they may keep distant from the amazement in which Paul has spoken of the matter. Who in fact can desire to hear any word on the subject other than this amazing one of Paul's? Ought not the extraordinary word of the Epistle to the Romans to be regarded as the only ordinary word on the subject? And was it therefore not inevitable that of all the apostles, amazing though it may appear, it was the figure of Paul that has from the very beginning impressed itself upon all Christendom as the figure of *the* Apostle. Can we avoid trying to come to an understanding, or, rather, associating ourselves with *the* Apostle of the Gospel not in spite of but because of the 'boldness' of his words? It may after all be possible that if we shun Paul's boldness we are finally and decisively shunning the Gospel itself.

15.22-33 speak of Paul's plans for the future. He would have visited the Church in Rome long before now (15.22; cf. 1.13). But many things – apparently his particular task too (in the sense of 15.20-21) have so far prevented him. Since he has now finished that tour (15.19), he wants to travel to Spain, visit the Church in Rome on his way, strengthen himself together with her (as was described in 1.11ff) and finally receive an escort from her midst for this further enterprise. But before that he must (15.25ff) undertake a journey in the opposite direction, to Jerusalem, personally to hand in the collection for the poor in Jerusalem which had been agreed upon and collected by the churches in Macedonia and Greece, which is discussed in detail in the Second Epistle to the Corinthians.

Note the motive for this collection given in 15.27: it is the material sign of the gratitude which is a matter of course to the Gentiles as regards people of Israel. By helping those who are materially poor they do not pay; they do however acknowledge the debt which they, the spiritually poor, owe them, the people of the Messiah who is the Saviour of the world. This is therefore not a charity like any other, but the adding of the seal – necessary for the foundation of the one Church of Jews and Gentiles – to the work of Paul. It is therefore something which he has to do himself. But when that is done, he will start the journey to Spain which will also bring him to Rome (15.28-29). He urges the church in Rome to accompany his journey to Jerusalem with her prayers. He will need them, for there, in the citadel of the unbelieving Synagogue in particular, he will encounter those who are 'disobedient'. He further does not seem to be so sure of such a good reception with the 'saints', with the Apostles and the other Christians of the original Church in Jerusalem, that he does not need this intercession.

According to II Cor. Paul had to win the Gentiles over to perform this act of gratitude cheerfully. In the same way he had to win over the Jewish Christians to satisfaction with his service as the Apostle of the Gentiles, and with this particular gesture. It was not a matter of course that they on their part would acknowledge the new relationship between Israel and the Church as revealed by the work of Paul, that they would accept its ratification by this collection in the way in which it was intended.

In 16.1-2 a Christian woman, Phoebe, is recommended to the hospitality of the church in Rome. It may be assumed that she took the Epistle from Corinth to Rome. She had so far been serving in the church at Cenchreae, the eastern seaport suburb of Corinth in some way, but we do not learn anything about the scope and character of her service. However, we are told that she has been a help to many, including Paul himself, and it is suggested to the Christians in Rome that they should reward her by any help she might need.

Now (16.3-15) follow Paul's private greetings to a whole number of individual members of the church in Rome who were known to him. It has been asked how it was possible for Paul to know so many people in this faraway church, and on this question as well as on certain details has been based the conjecture – already mentioned at the beginning of this work – that this list of greetings might be a letter or part of a letter addressed to another church which was better known to Paul (Ephesus has been suggested).

But if we take into account that in those days great numbers of people from all over the Mediterranean used to travel to Rome and settle there, it is not impossible that Paul actually did know many people in the Church who were old acquaintances from the East. However that may be, it is remarkable that, by means of this list of greetings, the Epistle to the Romans, which is the most objective of all Paul's letters, has at the same time received the most personal imprint. The majority of the people mentioned here are otherwise unknown to us. We know that Prisca and Aquila, the married couple mentioned in 16.3-4, crossed Paul's path more than once; however we do not know where and how they risked their lives for him, as stated in 15.4. Note the emphasis with which it is said that not only Paul but all the Gentile Christian churches too owe them a large debt of gratitude. The Rufus mentioned in 16.13 could be identical with the second son of Simon of Cyrene mentioned in Mark 15.21. As far as the others are concerned we have to be content with the little that is indicated here. The names mentioned in these verses can all be traced in contemporary inscriptions, and characteristically nearly all are names of slaves: an important hint concerning the social composition of this church and, according to I Cor. 1.26f, not only of this one. Aristobulus (16.10) and Narcissus (16.11), whose 'households' are greeted, are evidently Gentile lords in whose service those Christians were slaves. That the number of women is relatively large is as interesting as the fact that they are not a characteristic majority. One of them, the mother of Rufus (16.13) Paul called 'his mother and mine'. As Andronicus and Junias (16.7) and Herodion (16.11) are explicitly referred to as men of the same race as Paul, i.e. as Jews by birth we may infer that all the others are Gentiles by birth. We must note that in spite of all its 'boldness' the Epistle to the Romans has evidently not been 'too difficult' for these people. But objectively the most important thing is that as regards so many of those who are greeted (as for instance Phoebe, Prisca and Aquila are) – and particularly some of the women – it is accentuated that they have worked and laboured 'for you' or 'in the Lord' (16.6, 12). Urbanus is called Paul's fellow-worker (16.9) and Apelles 'the approved in Christ' (16.10). We cannot read this list of greetings without receiving the definite impression that all those 'beloved', 'elect' and 'saints' participated in the Gospel not merely receiving and enjoying it passively, and not merely being edified, taught, comforted and exhorted by it, but that they did this on their own responsibility, exertion and self-denial. The Gospel is just as much their concern as it is the Apostle's, and with this in mind he greets them and appeals to them as active fellow-workers in the same cause. The individuality is not submerged; it is fully honoured in the relationship between Apostle and Church. This happens in such a way that its real actuality is 'in the Lord', 'in Christ'; thereby is indicated once more not merely their presence but their general and particular co-operation.

Anyone who thinks that the Epistle to the Romans contains too much doctrine and too little life, too many words and too few works, should read this list of greetings and realize that the decision on the question of a life corresponding to the doctrine, of works corresponding to the words, lay then and still lies with the readers of the Epistle to the Romans. Those who care to ask that question should therefore first and foremost ask it of themselves. In Paul's day it was answered as positively as one can see from this list of greetings. Life is to be lived. Deeds are to be done. Where this happens in the way in which it evidently happened in Rome, there the other thing can and must apply: doctrine is to be taught and learned. But the converse must also be true: where doctrine is taught and learned as it was done here, life – which as such cannot very well be the contents of a letter – can and will be really lived.

In 16.16 Paul has evidently already started with the greetings which he has to forward from his surroundings: 'all the churches of Christ salute you.' Wherever the Gospel is preached evangelically, apostolically, the whole Church of all ages and all places greets the particular church which at that moment is called to hear it.

But before continuing with these greetings Paul interrupts himself (16.17-20) with a short, passionate warning against a temptation which threatens the Church in Rome, and which at the end (16.20) he does not hesitate to describe by the name of Satan. We do not know the particular reason for this warning, nor the particular character of the temptation here referred to. It is clear only that it concerns a deviation from the 'doctrine which you have learned', and the estrangement and scandal which could arise or had perhaps already arisen from that deviation – dangerous because its originators have the ability to present their cause with fair words and blessings ('fair speech' EVV). Who would not listen if something is in its way 'fair' and 'blessed'? The unsuspecting are then always prepared to mistake 'fair' for 'true' and 'blessed' for 'Christian'. When Paul says in 16.18 that those who threaten the Church in this pious way do not serve the Lord but their own belly, we ought certainly to understand this coarse expression politely, and therefore to the effect that what is here called the 'belly' also includes the heart and the head. So the 'belly' stands for the man who lives for his own sake and realizes his own life fully. That man is served and not Christ has been and is – from the point of view of the Epistle to the Romans – at all times the essence of all false doctrine, i.e. of all doctrine which is only apparently Christian. We have seen that the doctrine of the Epistle to the Romans does serve Christ. Any deviation from its doctrine will in fact mean serving man. This is therefore just what cannot be tolerated. Not in spite of but because of God's love it can on no account be tolerated. According to 16.19 Paul does not doubt that the Christians in Rome will remain faithful to the obedience which they have rendered so far. He does not worry about them, he rejoices in remembering them. But he wishes them the wise openness which they have need of to remain in their obedience – and the simple reserve which they need to ward off any possible disobedience. Note that what is at stake are not discussions and exchanges of opinion but only decisions, which moreover, will have to be taken 'shortly' (16.20) – decisions which the readers will have to make and in which nevertheless they have no choice. The God of peace, the Lord of the Church will decide, and their decision can only consist in their acknowledging that he has decided. Where the 'yes' of the Epistle to the Romans has once been spoken, there is obviously no need for much questioning to arrive at the 'no' to the reverse.

In 16.21-23 the greetings from Paul's acquaintances, which he had already wanted to begin in 16.16, find their place: Timothy, Paul's well-known fellow-worker, three Jewish-Christian friends, who are also known otherwise, Tertius who wrote the Epistle, Gaius with whom Paul is staying and in whose house the Corinthian church meets, Erastus, the treasurer of the city, evidently an honoured member of that church and an otherwise unknown brother Quartus.

The greeting in 16.20, repeated in 16.24: 'The grace of our Lord Jesus Christ be with you all!' sums up – here as well as in Paul's other letters – everything that he has to tell his Churches, all that he has to tell at all as an Apostle. The grace of our Lord Jesus Christ is the Gospel that Paul has preached and beside which according to Gal. 1.8 there is no other. The fact that the grace of our Lord Jesus Christ is with them is what makes the Christians Christians.

Here Paul's Epistle to the Romans ends. For what we find in 16.25-27 must for external and internal reasons be considered as a later addition by another hand. The contents of that addition are in themselves quite noteworthy, relevant and instructive, but we may refrain from explaining them, so that the last word in our ears is Paul's own: the very simple and very good word of the grace of our Lord Jesus Christ, which – this is his wish for his readers – may be with them all.

Index of Scripture References

Index of Scripture References